HERE AT
EAGLE POND

HERE AT
EAGLE POND

Donald Hall

ILLUSTRATIONS BY
THOMAS W. NASON

Ticknor & Fields
NEW YORK

For information about permission to reproduce selections
from this book, write to Permissions, Ticknor & Fields,
215 Park Avenue South, New York, New York 10003.

Library of Congress Cataloging-in-Publication Data
Hall, Donald.
Here at Eagle Pond / Donald Hall ; illustrations by Thomas W. Nason.
        p.   cm.
    ISBN 0–89919–978–x   ISBN 0–395–61154–7 (pbk.)
    1. Hall, Donald, 1928– — Homes and haunts — New Hampshire. 2. Poets,
American — 20th century — Biography. 3. New Hampshire — Social life and
customs. 4. Country life — New Hampshire.   I. Title.
            PS3515.A31522464   1990
                811'.54 — dc20
            [B]   90–37582
                        CIP

Printed in the United States of America

BP 10 9 8 7 6 5 4 3 2 1

The author and publisher wish to thank the family of Thomas W. Nason and
Margaret Warren Nason for permission to reproduce the illustrations.

The author is grateful to the following publications for permission to reprint the
material in this book: *Boston Globe:* The Rooster and the Silo. *Boston Globe Magazine:* The Fire That Never Went Out. *Country Journal:* Country Matters, Heman
Chase's Corners, Keeping Things. *Discover America!* (National Geographic Society):
My New England. *Esquire:* Why We Live Here. *Ford Times:* The Embrace of Old
Age, A Good Foot of Snow, Perennials. *Gettysburg Review:* Fifty People Talking
(reprinted, by permission of the editors, from *The Gettysburg Review*, vol. 3, no. 2).
Harper's Magazine: Living Room Politics (copyright © 1988 by *Harper's Magazine*,
all rights reserved, reprinted from the February issue by special permission). *New
England Journal of Public Policy:* Rusticus. *New England Monthly:* Reasons for
Hating Vermont. *New Hampshire Profiles:* Centuries of Cousins. *New York Times:*
The Radio Red Sox (copyright © 1986 by The New York Times Company, reprinted
by permission). *Yankee:* Good Use for Bad Weather, I ♥ My Dish, The Letter Farm,
October's Omens, The One Thousand Seasons. *The Walking Magazine:* To Walk a
Dog (reprinted with the permission of *The Walking Magazine*, 711 Boylston St.,
Boston, MA 02116, copyright © 1989).

In memory of Jack Jensen
and for Jo, Ruth, Janis,
Mark, and Kristina

CONTENTS

INTRODUCTION: THE LETTER FARM

In 1975 my wife and I moved from Michigan to Eagle Pond Farm in Wilmot, New Hampshire. For me, it was coming home, and it was coming home to the place of language. Years before, I had written a reminiscence, *String Too Short to Be Saved*, about the childhood summers when I hayed here with my grandfather. When I was twelve and thirteen, it was here that I began writing poetry. This farm provided subject matter for the first poems I published, when I was sixteen, and shows itself frequently in the two hundred and forty-four pages of *Old and New Poems*, collected in 1990 when I turned sixty-two. In 1986 I put together a book called *Seasons at Eagle Pond*. Now *Here at Eagle Pond* gathers other essays about this place that I have written over the past fifteen years. The relationship between essay and farm is symbiotic. Because I make my living by free-lance writing, magazines that ask me to write about Eagle Pond Farm help pay its mortgage. I have revised everything here, mostly to diminish repetition.* Still, this harvest of fifteen years remains diverse. I reprint a piece of largely objective prose cheek by jowl with sarcasms about Vermont and enthusiasms over New England weather. But these different voices are each my own voice — and

---

* Because I want *Here at Eagle Pond* to be complete in itself, I have repeated some details — church suppers, the Fourth of July — that turned up in *Seasons*.

Picasso said that every human being is a colony. Often books try to abide by a neoclassic unity of character; such a notion is unreal: On a given day, a woman or a man speaks in one voice (diction, syntax, gesture, tone) to the folks in the mailroom, in another to the CEO, in another when giving instructions to an assistant, in another to the same assistant met on the street, in another to spouse, in another to children.

Thinking of what I do, as I gather these essays together, I come upon an analogy that pleases me. My ancestors who lived here made their livings by free-lancing as farmers, by harvesting small crops for diverse markets. They raised chickens for eggs and meat, sheep for wool and meat, cattle for milk and meat; they raised vegetables, they cut timber, they harvested cider, maple syrup, and honey. They never accumulated much money, but they paid their taxes by the various products of their repeated labors. Thus I gather for the reader mutton, zucchini, apples, eggs, milk by the hundredweight, sweetness in two flavors — derived from trees and from insects — and a barrel of vinegar.

These essays are also letters to friends, and they become letters to strangers. When I left teaching and moved here, to support myself by writing, my friends were curious: How would we live? What would our lives be like, living here at Eagle Pond, in solitude among relics and memories, in a countryside of birches and GMC pickups? Some of these essays answered their questions, almost like those photocopied annual reports that people include with their Christmas cards. And some of these essays, I believe, climbed from the pages of real letters to friends.

My letter writing, real and metaphorical, came naturally enough out of my family. The women of Eagle Pond Farm worked as hard as the men did — an equality not of ownership or political rights but of toil. One relaxation in the women's long day was writing letters. My grandmother Kate Wells sat in the kitchen window to write daily letters to the three daughters who grew up at the farm just east of Eagle Pond, daughters who journeyed to far-off Lewiston, Maine, to attend Bates College, and who later moved to southern places: my mother Lucy to Connecticut, my aunt Caroline to Boston suburbs where she taught school, my aunt Nan to Northfield, New Hampshire. Sometimes

Kate's letters were postcards, a penny each, but she could pack a letter's worth onto the oblong with green Ben Franklin in the corner. Letters or postcards traveled south past Mount Kearsarge to daughters bearing news of *home*, for so she referred to Eagle Pond Farm, not for herself only but for her daughters, for her older sister Nannie, for her older brother Luther, and for her one grandchild. When she was past ninety she quizzed me elaborately to make sure that, in my absence from the farm — I was absent, then, three hundred and sixty-two days in the year — I referred habitually to·this place as home.

Returning letters arrived daily, exclaiming on the Eagle Pond weather report, carrying climate's intimate news — "The perspiration just *dripped* from my nose." "It was *glare ice*." — from the daughters of the diaspora back to the high priestess in her rocking chair. With her lips pursed in a scant smile, her brow furrowed, she concentrated reading her daughters' words. As an old woman, Kate never read anything *except* letters. Young, she was a student: Her report cards from Franklin High School, always quick to hand, demonstrated her A's in Greek, Latin, and everything else; but after she had graduated, at the end of the last century — or maybe after courtship and marriage and babies — she stopped reading. She darned and daydreamed in the evening while my grandfather reread *David Harum* and giggled.

Her only literature was letters, but what a letterist she was. Nor did it start with her. In the back chamber, in old chests and boxes along with diaries and slates and chalk and pens and dried inkwells, there are bundles of letters and postcards — Civil War letters, letters dispatched before stamps existed, letters of great formal intimacy often addressed to names I cannot place from names I cannot place. Nor did it end with her. I inherited the matter of Eagle Pond letters. I annoy my friends by answering their letters immediately. I puzzle publishers and magazine editors and impresarios of the poetry reading by writing instead of telephoning. I loathe the damned telephone; I prize the bundle of envelopes that Bruce (formerly Bert) leaves each day in the outsized mailbox. Every day is Christmas, as I settle back into my blue chair and hear my friends out, knowing that late in the day I will talk back to them. Last time I counted, I was talking (I dictate) four thousand letters and postcards a year. Our local p.o., suitably impressed, has rewarded me with a tribute I take as a postal knighthood: When you spell it out to nine digits, I have my own personal zip code. You could look it up; there's only one 03230–9599 in the universe. "Don Hall," it says.

If we go away for a week, the mail punishes us when we return. A few years back we left for seven weeks on a trip to China and Japan, and the mail that welcomed us home filled seven cardboard boxes. Travel can be a burden, but who wants to leave Eagle Pond anyway? My grandmother never did. Of course it takes all kinds, as we like to say. My grandmother's three girls all left, thus (*felix culpa*) providing her license to write them letters from Eagle Pond every day for fifty years. By pocket calculator (and mild exaggeration) that's 54,750 postal items. One of these daughters still fills the mailbox at Eagle Pond Farm, as my mother Lucy — residing in Connecticut exile at eighty-seven, looking more like Kate every day — lets us know by postcard and letter what the weather's like down there.

The first essay is "Why We Live Here," and so is the second, and so is the third . . . These pieces begin with the bliss of return, and toward the end of the book they add anxiety to joy. The predictable armies of development and overpopulation heave into sight on the southern and western horizons. Thus I join the chorus: *I got here. Everybody else stay out!* Sometimes when I praise where I live, in this old family house, I'm afraid that I sound like a cartoon that Herblock drew while Barry Goldwater was running for the presidency. Herblock had the senator snapping at a beggar, "Go inherit a department store." Reader, believe me: I know I am lucky. Every day, I know that my intimate connection with the family past, in this place, depends upon a series of accidents and not upon my virtue. Also I know that we do not require ancestors in order to connect, joyously, with a place and a culture. I see all around me emigrants from other places who belong more preciously to this place than most old-timers do. But I see as well — by looking afield to Nashua or Salem or Burlington — that overpopulation with its suburban density can disconnect us all from the land and its history.

17 March 1990

HERE AT
EAGLE POND

WHY WE
LIVE HERE

LATE SPRING and early summer, the whip-poor-will wakes us
at four-thirty. Gray light starts over the hills; thrushes sing from
every branch; clouds snag like lamb's wool on blue Mount Kearsarge. Down by Eagle Pond, just west of us, pickerel leap for
blackflies and when they splat on the still water wake frogs and
turtles. It is a good hour for waking; we keep the green universe
alone. But late September is the most beautiful time, and early
October, when it is dangerous to drive because you must not look
at the road. Sugar maples flare a Chinese red; they combine with
yellow birch leaves, russet oak, and evergreen to weave a wild
tweed on hills in the middle distance. I grant that winter causes
pain — in cold January sometimes I lie abed until six — but even
winter is gorgeous; when the moon is high, I wake at midnight
and wander through the farmhouse in gray, spooky light that
illuminates every corner, the ceilings luminous with reflections
from snowy hayfields.

We live where we live for landscape and seasons, for the place
of it, but also for the time of it, daily and historical time. Although I keep a farmer's hours I farm no crops. Ancestors who
took their turns inhabiting this house arose to milk cattle, to feed
hens and sheep. I work on paper at my desk, in the room where
I slept as a child — and I live here because it was my grandpar-

ents' place, which sets me into the decades. The original Cape was 1803. My sheep-farmer great-grandfather sold wool for uniforms, and in 1865 bought this valley farm next to the railroad, moving down from his steep Ragged Mountain acreage. Where once he pastured his merinos, now cables drag flatlanders uphill, wearing petroleum by-products with a dollar value that would have sounded like riches in 1865.

We live here also for the solitude. Friends drive up from New York, admire the landscape, swim in the pond, wear us out, and as they are leaving ask, clearing their throats, "But, uh, what do you *do?*" Sometimes we wish we had a little *more* solitude. Maybe because we both write poetry, we are untroubled by the notoriety that hides J. D. Salinger behind fences up in Cornish . . . But occasionally somebody seeks us out. A few years back I heard a knock on the front door, through which nothing has entered or exited, except for corpses, since 1865. Two readers from California had tracked me down. The bold one took me out to the car, to meet the shy one, who congratulated me (before I detached myself to return to my desk) "on your privacy and seclusion."

We did not come here for the social life, yet we found enough. We had not been here long before Jane found the word for Thornley's store, the general store just out of sight around a bend: Thornley's is a continual party. Go there any time of day and somebody is telling a story. At Thornley's you learn that it got so cold last week that Ansel saw two hound dogs putting jumper cables on a jackrabbit. At Thornley's you learn who's getting divorced, and maybe why; you talk politics, weather, old times, and what's for dinner down to the Grange in town.

"Town" is ambiguous. It is difficult, in the country, to give a straight answer when somebody asks where you live. Haying with my grandfather when I was a boy, I considered that we lived in West Andover because that was our post office. Now West Andover is gone except for houses, and our post office is Danbury. The telephone exchange, however, is Andover; we call the Danbury p.o. long-distance. On the other hand, Wilmot is the town of our town meeting, and the town to which we pay our taxes. Wilmot is composed of Wilmot Center, Wilmot Flat, and North Wilmot — little centers mostly gone where West Andover went. We live in a flap of the town that tucks over Route 4 between Danbury and Andover, a flap that a hundred years ago called itself East Wilmot, but never acquired the depot, inn, livery stable, fishmonger, butcher, and two grocery stores that made West Andover a quondam metropolis.

Besides continual parties like the store, there are special ones. South Danbury Christian Church, where I find myself deacon, has a coffee hour every Sunday. (Attendance has vaulted in nine years,* from an average of ten to an average of twenty.) Most towns specialize in one annual holiday. The most elaborate local celebration is Andover's Fourth of July. Last year it began with a pancake breakfast at seven, put on by the Lions Club. The flea market, art show, and midway got started a little later — hundreds of crafters with leather and ceramics, tables of junk, turtle races, hot dogs — before the parade at noon. Past the bandstand marched the Shriners' band, kids rolled decorated bicycles, floats celebrated American Pastimes, fire engines first-geared, a dozen old cars shone like new dimes, pickups crowded with Babe Ruth League teams slowed by — and riders on horseback, and a farmer leading oxen, and seven clowns throwing candy to children. Afternoon featured a town baseball game, pony pulling, and a guitar player.

Until last year, the midway continued into darkness; for years I worked the booth where you throw soggy baseballs at wooden bottles, twenty-five cents for three balls, and if you knock down the bottles I give you a ten-cent prize. (This concession was property of the Andover Lions Club, of which I used to be a dilatory member.) At dark there were fireworks, but the year before last, some lout let off a canister of tear gas during fireworks, which ended the fireworks.† Last year Andover's Fourth concluded with a barbecue chicken dinner, five to seven P.M., put on by the Volunteer Fire Department.

Of the three towns we live in, Danbury is my favorite because it is the wildest, with most diversity of character, many eccentrics,

---

* I wrote this essay in 1984. I have not tried to bring my figures up to date.

† 1990. They have returned.

and a few louts. The diversity of the country is its greatest quality, and nowhere outside the East Village of Manhattan are
people so various as in Danbury, New Hampshire — lazy and
industrious, rich and poor, aged and precocious, virtuous and
wicked. Because much of the younger set is shaggy, with long
hair and untended beards, the word "hippie" finds an afterlife
here. In Danbury Center, across from Dick's Store, there is an
elevated strip of land between Route 4 and the railroad, where
trains no longer run. Someone has spread wood chips, and there's
a trash can, and some trash chairs and milkcases to sit on. Here
a portion of Danbury youth, up to the age of forty, spends mild
summer evenings drinking Dick's six-packs and smoking hand-
rolled cigarettes. This informal, privately operated recreation
area is known as Hippie Hill.

Danbury Center includes the Grange, two churches, and two
stores. Every September after Labor Day, Danbury's annual bash
is the Danbury Grange Harvest Festival Parade. By 1983, without many farmers left, maybe it celebrates harvesting the summer people, who are tucked back in the suburbs by this time. The
American Legion Hall swells with prize vegetables, the Grange
Hall with brownies and antiques for sale, and with the work of
local watercolorists. There are hamburgers and hot dogs for
lunch, and in the evening a big dinner at the Grange. The parade
features fire engines hooting — the same that rolled on Andover's
Fourth, without hooting in staid Andover — a fife and drum corps
from Bristol, Willard Huntoon's brace of Holstein oxen, and
floats representing organizations; sometimes I ride in the back
of a yellow Datsun pickup, the deacon waving from the South
Danbury Christian Church Sunday School float. There is also a
float labeled Hippie Hill, which features young folk lolling on
cut grass drinking six-packs at ten-thirty on a Saturday morning
in September.

Between our house and Danbury Village, South Danbury is
another disappearing town, whose remaining identity resides
mostly in the white clapboard church that my great-grandparents helped to start after the Civil War. When we moved here
nine years ago we decided that *they* — probably the dead —
would expect us to go to church . . . Wearily we dragged our-

selves there the first Sunday; the second Sunday we went less wearily; within a few weeks we got there early. Let me not go into theology. Let me mention that our minister — Jack Jensen from Kansas City and Yale Divinity, who teaches at Colby-Sawyer College nearby — the first Sunday quoted Rainer Maria Rilke. Although the allusion pleased us, it was not excerpts from German poets that turned us into deacons. It started with community, and extended itself to communion. One side of the church, which Jane calls the gene pool, shares a couple of great-grandparents, but the true community is an extraordinary interconnectedness. We cover much social territory — age, occupation, politics, tone deafness — and we are also connected to the community of the dead, who lie in the graveyard up the road, and to the unborn. Funerals, weddings, and baptisms mark sensible boundaries.

Our annual festival is the South Danbury Church Fair. Early in July, three o'clock one Saturday afternoon, we start with tables of white elephants, food, fancywork, books, and clothing. We sell homemade ice cream, pop, and grabs for the kids. After supper we hold an auction. The major labor is the church supper, which starts at five P.M., costs ludicrously little, and includes beans, ham, meat loaf, turkey salad; lasagna and twenty other casseroles; bread, rolls, salads, and fifty pies.

Magnificent. Also exhausting for the dozen women who especially labor at it. *Mostly* women. For the past eight years I have created meat loaves, turkey salads, and American chop sueys, breaking the sex barrier at the South Danbury Church Fair. Actually, as I discover, the barrier had already been broken — but movement out of the kitchen closet had been covert: The delicious rolls of my cousin Edna (who cooks many casseroles, who makes annually a famous bright red velvet cake) are really the work of her husband Ansel.

Two hundred eat dinner, and fifty or so stay on for the auction. Bill McKenzie is auctioneer, with helpers who display items, fetch, deliver, and accept cash payment. Bill sells a feather mattress, eighteen Venetian blinds, old china, boxes of *Reader's Digest* condensed books, a 1939 *Encyclopedia Americana*, three plastic draining trays for dishes, forty-two worn LPs of Johnny

Cash, outgrown jackets, pies unconsumed at dinner, leftover sliced ham, a tattered sofa, a banjo with a missing string, window shades, purses, hats, pots, pans, trays, bathroom cabinets, kitchen chairs, a bridge table, a tricycle, and forty-seven busted plastic children's toys.

Bill's voice fills the little hillside next to the church as he spiels down to neighbors gathered at the foot of the slope, some resting on folding chairs they brought with them. He keeps a straight face but no one else does. His helper, my cousin Forrest, who is beefy and strong, annually dons a woman's hat and swings a pocketbook as he models items for auction. Cousin bids against cousin and brother against sister, driving the prices up to dizzying heights — two dollars, two and a half, two seventy-five. Always a few strangers, among the throng of old familiars, get caught up. Last summer I changed a hundred-dollar bill from the billfold of a New Yorker, the first recorded C-note in the history of the South Danbury Christian Church.

Finally, we live where we live mostly because of a weird mixture: permitted solitude and strong society. Many Danbury families find their surnames on the bronze plaque outside the Town Hall that lists veterans of the Civil War, but others moved here last week; it makes little difference in Danbury. People move here because they want to live here — they don't come here for the wages, nor do companies transfer managers to Danbury — and people born here do not move away, to seek their fortunes, *only* because they want to live here. We associate in the shared love of place and in an ethic. When X's house burns down — say, someone widely disliked, a leading local Snopes — twelve pickups deliver household goods the next morning. It is what you do. You *are* your brother's keeper; you do it without needing to think about it, because it is an ethic that goes with the place.

Of our three towns, Danbury is the most country and the least Vermont. Heaven knows, Vermont is a beautiful state, with pockets of real country remaining, but it is the chic northern New England rural retreat, and not New Hampshire. To Vermont go summering professors of philosophy and Dada poets from New Jersey. The result is Woodstock, where orthopedic surgeons wear checkered shirts from L. L. Bean and play at being country folk. Alas, patches of New Hampshire already approach Vermonthood. We have heard the sound of condosaurus slapping its beaverboard tail in distant meadows. Maybe one day Danbury will be digested by Yankee suburbia, and on Route 4 will arise boutiques, disguised as saphouses, that feature Venetian glass. By that time, I will have joined my ancestors down the road, and together we will haunt skiers and golfers with chain-rattling ectoplasm.

KEEPING
THINGS

The Back Chamber

On the second floor of our house there is a long, unfinished room that my family has always called the back chamber. It is the place the broken chair ascends to when it is too weak for sitting on; the broken lamp finds its shelf there, the toolbox its roost after the carpenter's death. You do not throw things away: You cannot tell when they might come in handy. My great-grandfather was born in 1826 and died in 1914; some of his clothes remain in the back chamber, waiting to come in handy.

His name was Benjamin Keneston, and he had two sons and three daughters, the youngest my grandmother Kate, who died at ninety-seven in 1975. Most of Ben's children were long-lived; when they survived their spouses they would come home, bringing a houseful of furniture with them. They never called this place anything but home, or used the word for any other place, though they might have lived and worked elsewhere for fifty years. Both Luther and Nannie returned to live in cottages near the farm, and Kate kept bedrooms at the house in their names — Luther's room, Nannie's room — for when they were sick. Their extra furniture went to the back chamber, or above the back chamber in a loft, or in the dark hole that extends under eaves in the old part of the house without windows or electric lights.

When we potter in the back chamber today, we find a dozen knocked-down double beds, one painted with gold designs and the slogan *Sleep Balmy Sleep* on dark veneer. We find something like thirty chairs: captain's chairs, rockers with a rocker missing, Morris chairs, green painted kitchen chairs, pressed-wood upright dining room chairs, uncomfortable stuffed parlor chairs; most of them lack a strut or a leg but live within distance of repair. We find a sewing machine that my grandmother sewed on for sixty years and a 1903 perambulator she wheeled my mother in. Two sisters came after my mother, and the back chamber is well furnished with dolls' furniture: tiny chests of drawers, small rockers and small captain's chairs, prams, cradles, and a miniature iron cookstove, like the big Glenwood range in the kitchen below, with an oven door that swings open, firebox, stove lids, and a tiny iron skillet that fits a stovetop opening. We find fat old wooden skis and sleds with bentwood runners. One ancient stove, with castiron floral reliefs, we cleaned up and use in Jane's study, which used to be Nannie's room. We find toolboxes, post card collections, oil lamps, electric lamps, pretty cardboard boxes, books by Joe Lincoln and Zane Grey, cribs, carpetbags, loveseats, and a last for making shoes. We find three spinning wheels, two of them broken and a third intact, dispatched upstairs when Ward's replaced homespun; as the family remembers, Benjamin's wife Lucy Buck Keneston was a wonderful spinner. We find a dozen quilts too frail for cleaning, showing bright squares of the cut-up dresses of seamstresses born to the early Republic. We find six or seven chests full of dead people's clothing, Ben Keneston's among them. In a dark row stand four baby highchairs; one made from stout brown wood is more than seventy years old, first used by my mother's younger sister Nan, next by me, later by my children; two wicker highchairs are older, and a frail wooden one older still. I don't know which of them my grandmother sat in.

In the back chamber we keep the used and broken past. Of course it is also a dispensary. When my daughter moved from her University of New Hampshire dormitory to an apartment in Dover, she outfitted her flat from unbroken furniture out of the back chamber. With glue and dowels, the apartments of children and grandchildren could be filled for fifty years. In, and out again: the past hovering in the dusty present like motes, a future implicit in shadowy ranks of used things, usable again. We do not call these objects antiques; they were never removed from use as testimony to affluence. Twice a year, as I show somebody through the house, somebody decides that I am in need of counseling: "You've got a fortune here." I keep my temper. None of it would fetch a great price, but even if it would, I would as soon sell my ancestors' bones for soup as I would sell their top hats, chairs, tool chests, and pretty boxes. Someday when we are dead let them go to auction, if they are not repaired and dispersed.

Continually we discover new saved things, and my wonder is not for the things themselves but for the saving of them. Could Kate really have thought, when she put away a 1917 agricultural bulletin, that it might come in handy someday? The back chamber bespeaks attachment to the outlived world. On a long, narrow cardboard box an old hand has written, "Wool was from B. C. Keneston's sheep carded and ready for spinning at Otterville" — where there was a carding mill — "in 1848." When we open it, we find protected by mothballs a few pounds of one-hundred-and-forty-year-old sheep's wool, preserved for preservation's sake, so that we may touch our fingers to the wool our ancestor's fingers sheared. (Was 1848 his first crop from his first sheep? He was twenty-two that year.) This back chamber is like the parlor walls covered with family portraits, like the graveyard with its Vermont slate and New Hampshire granite; it keeps the dead.

The Saphouse

When we moved into the old house after my grandmother's death, it needed work. (She was seventy-four when my grandfather died. He had kept the house up, and after his death she could not afford to hire help. My mother paid to keep the house painted and the roof dry.) Now as we painted and shingled, dug out the cesspool, planted daffodils, put in a leachfield, fertilized hayfields, jacked up the woodshed for a new sill, replaced clapboards, and mulched old roses, our neighbors let us know that they were pleased. In this countryside, everyone over fifty had watched white wooden houses lose paint and tilt inward as their roofs sagged, and finally whole square-built houses collapse into their own cellarholes. Everyone here takes interest in preserving things, in landscape and buildingscape, even if everyone knows that in a hundred years fire will consume all these houses.

One outbuilding was too far gone for us to bring it back. Built at the turn of this century just north of the house, the saphouse had been the site of prodigious syrup making. In 1913 my grandfather, with the help of his father-in-law and Freeman Morrison,* made five hundred gallons to sell for a dollar each, and put the windfall into land. Because it takes about forty gallons of sap to make a gallon of syrup — the pale sap is watery; it is hard to taste the sweetness — he hauled twenty thousand gallons of maple sap that year, in the two or three weeks of sugaring. First he tapped the huge old trees of the sugarbush on Ragged Mountain, setting one or more buckets at each tree to collect the dripping liquid; then he visited each tree each day, emptying the buckets into twenty-gallon pails he carried on a yoke across his shoulders; then he walked through the snowy woods to the ox sledge, where he poured the sap into milk cans; when the cans were full he eased his oxen to a funnel uphill from the saphouse and piped his crop down to the saphouse's holding tank.

When I was little and visited the farm in March, if I hit upon sugaring time, I walked the sugarbush with him. The crop is best when days are warm and nights freezing. To keep the sap boiling, somebody has to tend the fire twenty-four hours a day; Freeman, who was a night owl, stayed up all night and much of the day to feed the fire. He pushed whole trees, foot by foot, over the snow through the saphouse's open doors into the firebox. Freeman and my grandfather had built the saphouse under the supervision of my grandfather's father-in-law, informally called Uncle Ben. (Formally he was Benjamin Cilley Keneston, to distinguish

---

* Freeman was my grandmother's cousin, brought up almost as a sibling. In *String Too Short to Be Saved* I called him Washington Woodward; the protagonist of my children's book *The Man Who Lived Alone* is modeled on Freeman.

him from his father, who was plain Benjamin. When I was a child I liked knowing that I was part Cilley.) BCK died in 1914, sixty-six years after he sheared the sheep's wool in the back chamber. Although I never knew him, I have been aware of his presence since I was a child, and living in his house I feel him every day, not only in the photograph on the living room wall or the top hat under the stairs. If we find a tar-brand for sheep it is *K*. He was diminutive and powerful, and it must have been hard for my grandfather Wesley Wells to marry his daughter, move into his house, and take direction from him. Yet I never caught a shade of resentment in the stories my grandfather told me.

We hated to pull the saphouse down. My grandfather used it last to make a few gallons in March 1950. That autumn he had a heart attack, sold the cows, and never used the saphouse again. He died in March 1953. When we moved into his house in 1975 we found an unopened quart from his last crop of syrup on a shelf in the rootcellar. Maybe if I had been truest to family practices I would have carried it up to the back chamber unopened but labeled for future generations to wonder at. However, we opened it, we ate it on pancakes, and when we had almost finished it, we poured the last drops into a store-bought gallon — figuring that for a few decades at least, if we continued emptying old gallons into new ones, we could imagine molecular survival for my grandfather's final quart.

The saphouse leaned over, a third out of the vertical. The shed-like door gapped loose. I no longer entered it, because sometime the roof would collapse and I would not let it collapse on me. Rot feathered the timbers up from the ground, the tarpaper roof was swaybacked, and the lead pipe sagged as it rose up-mountain from the rotten galvanized holding tank. Twenty years before, my grandmother Kate had sold the evaporator — big tin tray over the firebox — to somebody building a new saphouse; somebody else had bought the buckets. Every now and then, a pickup braked in front of the house and a stranger offered to tear the saphouse down for us, in return for the old wood that he could salvage. There's a market for old wood: beams for what is called restoration, planks to be cut up for picture frames. I refused these offers, wanting to keep the old wood, and probably because I inherited or acquired the desire to keep things. Also I remembered the sheepbarn. Two men tore it down for my grandmother when it started to lean over; they promised, as all the pickup people promised, to clean it up real good. But when these fellows had removed the solid wood they left a mess of rotten board and shingle that weeds grew to cover, a treacherous vegetal-archaeo-logical heap you could break a leg in, where woodchucks bred for generations until we hired a dozer and a truck to haul the mess to the dump.

We tied a cable around the saphouse walls, hitched the cable to a four-wheel-drive pickup, and pulled it down. The frail boards stretched apart like a clasped bunch of straw when you unclench your fist. Sun touched bright unweathered boards that had seen no light since Wesley and Freeman lifted them from the saw-mill's pile and hammered them in place. Store nails pulled from the corner four-by-fours. At the door we found long, irregular hammered iron pins, which Freeman had pounded out at his forge in the shop that stood not twenty yards away — the shop also gone now, all traces gone except the grindstone's base that leaned beside it.

We tossed rotten boards in the pickup's bed, stacked the good wood and hauled it for storage to the cowbarn with its kept-up roof. At day's end we drove the junk to the town dump. In a wheelbarrow we collected old bottles, one intact sap bucket, a float, an enamel funnel, and an elegantly shaped handmade shovel. Two huge tapered iron hinges bore a hammer's prints. We tucked the ironwork in a corner of the woodshed (where fire-wood covers it half the year) among ax heads, scythe blades, and the frail graceful trident of a pitchfork. Freeman forged some of this iron with his engineering-generalist's skill — who turned baseball bats on a lathe, tanned leather and made shoes, built lad-ders and hayricks and playhouses and wooden spoons and stone walls, repaired cutlery and milk pails, moved rocks and pulled stumps — but some of the work is finer than Freeman's; I fancy the hand of John Wells, Wesley's father, who fought at Vicks-burg and returned to be blacksmith and farrier on a hill west of Danbury.

Soon grass and saplings would cover the debris we left behind, bricks and small pieces of wood, chowder of rusted metal, spread now in a drift of old leaves that blew into the saphouse autumns past, gray-brown and fragile. High in the center stood the one monument that remained like the saphouse's tombstone, the long brick hive of fire, firebox into which Freeman had pushed whole trees. Seventy-five-year-old mortar spilled at the edge of bricks pink as a baby's mouth. I remember hearing that BCK liked to butter bricks; he must have done this work. Maybe in a hundred years a hiker walking down Ragged Mountain will find this brickwork among new maples.

When we were done, birches cast late-day shadows across the little field between the house and the place where the saphouse used to be. Then we noticed an odd-shaped white stone where there had been a corner four-by-four. It was flat and looked carved. We lifted it up and saw that beneath it there was another piece just like it, and when we turned the top one over, we understood two things at once: The two pieces fitted where they had broken in the middle, and it was a tombstone. Cleaning it off, I read the name and dates of my great-great-grandfather, BCK's father, BENJAMIN KENISTON 1789–1863. Because I knew his grave in the old Andover graveyard, because I remembered the sturdy, legible stone above it, I understood that this was his *first* gravestone, that it had broken, that his son BCK had replaced it — and brought it home and put it to use.

The Bone Ring

The first month we moved here, going through an old desk, we found a yellowed piece of stationery headed by an indistinct photograph of Mount Kearsarge and the words *B. C. Keneston Eagle Pond Farm*. (It was BCK who changed the spelling of the family name, to distance himself from some Keniston cousins.) The pond is west of the farm, thirty acres of water — a lake anywhere else. No one alive remembered that name for the place. Although it had not stuck, I decided to make use of it, not for piety of reference but to ease the minds of urban and suburban correspondents who find it hard to believe that a town's name can be address enough. So BCK solved a problem: All that first year, the dead helped out.

Mostly they demanded attention. I could not decide whether Freeman or BCK demanded more. (My grandparents, whom I knew so well and loved so much, demanded little; I thought of them without being reminded.) BCK, whom I had never known, had picked this place out; it was he who deserved credit for staking the claim to Kearsarge and to Eagle Pond. It was he who bought the pew at the South Danbury church he helped to found, where his daughter Kate played the organ Sundays from the age of fourteen to ninety-two. (Is seventy-eight years at the same organ a neo-Calvinist record?) It was fitting, then, that my one glimpse of his ghost, looking suspiciously like my favorite photograph of him, occurred in church one Sunday. He vanished as soon as I saw him. If every Sunday I caught sight of my grandmother's black sequined hat, bobbing next to the green glass lampshade above the organ, that vision seemed natural enough.

Freeman insisted on his presence in a manner perfectly material. He had stenciled his name all over the house. Cousin Freeman moved in as a boy when his family was burned out; he preferred Uncle Ben and Aunt Lucy to his parents and loved Kate like a little sister. His father took him away and put him to work when he was sixteen, but for the rest of his life he kept returning to this place that he loved. I remember him old and sick, wrapped in a blanket, tucked into the rocker by the kitchen range, attended

by Kate grown old. He stenciled his name on the underside of
stairs leading to the back chamber, which we could see as we
walked down to the rootcellar. He stenciled his name on the bottom of a drawer in the pantry, on the underside of the windowsill
in his room, and on shingles we found wedged under a box in the
toolshed. When we turned something over or lifted something up,
we half expected to see Freeman's name, as if his face with its
playful eyes leapt up like a jack-in-the-box. He stenciled his
name, as it were, on everybody who knew him.

My ghost stories are mostly unconscious memory. When we
had lived here only a few weeks a stranger knocked on the front
door; his trailer had broken down and he needed a large monkey
wrench. I started to say that I had no big wrench, but before I
could speak something took hold of me. Asking the man to wait
I gave myself over to whatever possessed me and let it direct me
out of the kitchen, into the toolshed toward the woodshed door;
my right hand rose unbidden toward a flat shelf over that door
where the big wrench resided, and had resided forever, covered
now with thirty years of dust and spider webs. Something similar
happened when I bought a sickle at Thornley's store to chop down
weeds in the barnyard. I cut Lexington plant until my back
stopped me, then walked with my silvery crescent into the toolshed where I would find something to hang it on; I did not know
why I headed for a particular place, but when I raised my hand
toward the naily ceiling, I saw three frail rusted sickles hanging
there already.

Not everything that happened was memory. Once my wife
heard her name called repeatedly in the barn when no one was
there to say it. Once after someone helping us cleaned a shed loft,
and threw away old shoes and clothing we would not have
thrown away, Jane felt in the loft some violence, anger, or even
evil, as if something terrible had happened there; maybe it was
only resentment over things lost. And there was something else
soon after we moved in, although we did not hear about it for
two years. It happened to a visitor — skeptical, secular, unsuper-
stitious, hesitant to speak of it, unable to understand what she
saw. It was just a *seeing*. As she stood in our living room, she saw
someone in the doorway of the kitchen, someone who was not

there: a short man, bearded, wearing overalls and a hat. Both BCK and Freeman were short, bearded, wore overalls and a hat.

These experiences virtually stopped after that first year, but there was an exception. When we had lived here six years, we finally afforded a new bathroom. The old one was Sears 1937: cold, shabby, showerless. We tore it off the side of the house and put a new bathroom (with shower and laundry) into our old bedroom, extending a new bedroom onto the north lawn. For warmth in winter we extended the rootcellar under the new room, which obliged us to raise the north side of the house on jacks and bulldoze underneath it. We dug out rotten sills and replaced them; ripping a wall from the old bedroom we exposed 1803 carpentry; the wallpaper of the family Troy was nine layers deep; in one wall we found cardboard insulation from a box of breakfast cereal, Washington's Crisps, and a picture of the general with bright red lips.

It was the first major alteration of the house's shape since BCK expanded it in 1865, when it became the extended farmhouse familiar in New Hampshire — outbuildings not separated but linked one to one, moving in slow file backward to the hill. To haul firewood in winter we pass through a kitchen door into the toolshed, which is another repository almost like the back chamber: saws, levels, crowbars, old nails, screws, bolts, shovels, rakes, hoes, sickles, awls, drills and their bits, hammers, hammerheads, traps, stovepipe, lanterns, wrenches, screwdrivers; and the practice organ Kate learned to play on, moved from the parlor to the toolshed in 1927 when my mother and father displayed wedding presents in the parlor — and at the southeast corner of the toolshed we go through another door into the woodshed. This door is made from planks nailed to crossplanks, and it latches by a smooth oblong of wood — touched ten million times like Saint Peter's toe to a soft and shiny texture — which turns on a bolt and sticks at a thumb of wood below. Because we must carry wood many times a day, much of the year, we have unfixed the latch to open this door thousands of times, walked into the woodshed, loaded up with logs, and walked back out again, latching the door behind us. But while we were tearing things up, something new happened, not once or twice but seven times: While we were fetching logs, this woodshed door swung closed behind us, and the wooden latch turned by itself and locked us inside the woodshed.

It never happened once in the years before; in the years since we stopped sawing and hammering, it has not happened again. This locking up was not malicious, because it is easy enough to get out of the woodshed by a door that leads outside. Not malicious, just an annoying prank.

The steadiest presence remains in the possessions, rooms, and artifacts of the dead. Living in their house, we take over their practices and habits, which makes us feel close to them and to the years that they knew. I always wanted to live in this house with the old people, and now I do, even though they are dead. I don't live in their past; they inhabit my present, where I live as I never lived before. I used to survive, like many people, half in a daydream of future reward that is a confession of present malaise: the vacation trip, the miraculous encounter. When I moved here, at first I feared the fulfillment of desire, as if I would be punished for possessing what I wanted so much; there was a brief time when I drove ten miles under the speed limit and buckled up to move the car in the driveway; but contentment was relentless and would not let me go until I studied the rapture of the present tense. It turns out that the fulfillment of desire is to stop desiring, to live in the full moon and the snow, in the direction the wind comes from, in the animal scent of the alive second.

The dead were welcoming. I worried about usurping their place until two dreams helped me. In one I discovered that my grandfather — who was working the farm, now, in my dream — had disappeared and I thought him dead, only to see him striding up the dirt road from Andover (a road paved before I was born), leading a file of zoo animals: ostrich, bear, elephant, lion, tiger. He had traded the cows and sheep for these exotic creatures, proving (as I take the dream) that I was permitted to raise poems on this farm instead of stock. The other dream was more to the point of disappearances; a large voice pronounced, "The blow of the ax resides in the acorn."

If there is no connected past, we lack the implication of persistence after our own death. The preserved or continuous past implies the possibility that oneself may continue, in place or object or even in spirit, a ring of time that revolves, revisits, and contains. As a child I heard about a bone ring. When John Wells fought at Vicksburg he stood next to a young man named George Henry Butler, who came from a farm on New Canada Road; people from the same neighborhoods fought together in that war. As they were shelled, Wells took cover behind a great tree, which allowed him to stand upright; Butler squatted in a hole beside him. When the cannonade continued Wells offered to switch places with Butler, to let him stretch for a bit, and when they had changed places, a cannonball crashed through the tree and took off the young man's head. My great-grandfather emptied Butler's pockets, and when he mustered out and walked home to Danbury turned over the dead soldier's possessions to his family.

John Wells's son Wesley married George Henry Butler's cousin Kate Keneston, and one object from those pockets came down to her. A few years ago it disappeared. No one could find it in the house, and we thought it was gone forever. We lamented the lost connection with a young man killed in the Civil War. Then we discovered it in a box of buttons in the back chamber: a finger ring carved out of bone, eight-sided, scratched with little decorations, small and yellowed — a bone ring I take as emblem of this place.

Here are some brief essays that I wrote after I first came back, full of the ecstasy of return. Some are about living here now, and some are recollections. To live here, in any now, is to occupy a present gaily continuous with a past.

PERENNIALS

I LIVE IN the house I always wanted to live in. When I was a boy, spending summers here with my grandmother and grandfather, I wrote poems and read books in the morning; in the afternoon I hayed with my grandfather, listening to his long, slow stories of old times. I loved him, and he gave me the past of his boyhood as if it were a fortune or a mild chronic disease. Over the years of separation, in a suburban world, I felt continuously connected with this land and with the dead who make it precious. Now I return full circle, except that I write all day and I do not hay at all. If I miss my grandfather and his stories, I do not miss him so much as I used to; he died long ago but he is no longer *missing*. As I reach the age he carried when I was born, I sleep in the bed he died in and I find him everywhere I look. In a cousin's cheekbone, in a turn of phrase, in a remembered quilt I find him.

Paul Fenton reminds me of my grandfather, with good reason. Paul's mother was Wesley's sister Grace, who died just three years ago. Paul is seventy now, a pacemaker in his chest, and he complains that although he can still chop wood all day, now he must pause sometimes to catch his breath, and the doctor can't tell him why. When I was a boy on the farm, my grandfather was in his sixties and seventies, while Paul was early in middle age. Paul and Bertha used to call on Wesley and Kate; my grandfather saved good stories for Paul, who liked hearing his uncle's talk. Now sometimes Bertha and Paul will call on us, driving over from the long farm where their son Dennis keeps fifty Holsteins, and Paul has a story to tell me.

When Paul was a boy, an old man told him this one, and the old man told Paul that he had heard it from an old man when *he* was a boy.

"So this one goes back some . . .

"Once there was a man living around here who filled his ox cart every year in the fall.* He filled it with everything he and his family made over the whole year: things his wife and daughters sewed or knitted or crocheted, things like yarn and cloth, goose feathers for stuffing beds, linen and flax seed. Probably the man and his boys made shingles he put in the ox cart; young boys made birch brooms. And he put in the ox cart everything from his fields that would keep and that he didn't need: extra apples, potatoes, Indian corn, turnips, pumpkins, and squash; vinegar, honey in combs, dried meat, and maybe tanned deerhide.

"Well, he filled it right up with everything all of them had made or done or grown, leaving behind just enough for them to eat and wear all winter. Then he walked beside his ox, ten days maybe, all the way to Portsmouth, where there was a big market. (One year he went all the way down to Boston, to the market by the harbor.) When he got to market he sold whatever he had. There'd be sailors in Portsmouth then, and people came from all around to do their shopping. After he sold his potatoes he sold the bag he brought the potatoes in. If he had vinegar in a barrel, you know he'd've made the barrel too; so then he sold the barrel.

---

* After I heard Paul's story, I spent two years making a poem called "Ox-Cart Man," which I printed in *Kicking the Leaves;* I changed one word for *Old and New Poems.* When I had finished the poem I told the same story, in different words, to make the children's book *Ox-Cart Man,* which Barbara Cooney illustrated and which won her the Caldecott Medal in 1981. In "Keeping Things" I told about building a new bathroom. It was expensive, and over its door I've set a plaque: *Caldecott Room.*

When he sold everything out of his cart, and the cart was empty, he sold the cart. After he sold the cart he sold his ox, harness and all."

Paul pauses a moment, grinning, and looks at me to see how I like his story's twist. I like it. Paul goes on.

"Then he walked home. Maybe he bought things for his family with the money. Salt, an orange for each of them — they never saw oranges in those days — maybe needles or knives, things he couldn't make at his own forge. But he had his year's money, money for the year.

"Then when he came home he started everything over again, the young ox in the barn, the harness, the cart . . ."

Paul smiles, excitement in his face; he knows what he has given. Soon he must stand and leave, back to the chores by which he helps Dennis, his necktie and white shirt back in the closet until Sunday. He will wear overalls again, become farmer again — winter and summer, garden and cattlebarn.

He leaves me to early November nightfall and my dream of the ox-cart man. I see him walking home from Portsmouth Market, up Highway 4 from Concord through Penacook, Boscawen, Salisbury, Andover. On a narrow dirt road he walks steadily, coins heavy in his pockets, past forest and farm, pasture and cornfield, big houses and settlers' cabins. Now he walks through West Andover, almost home, and I see him down the road in the cool afternoon sun, slanting low from Vermont, lengthening shadows of cornstalks blackened with frost. Now he is home — it is this farm, as I dream it — and his family gathers around him as he gives each of them a gift from his great pockets, needles and combs for the women, a Barlow knife for each boy, and stashes the cash in the treasury crock, which he keeps under a stone in the rootcellar. Now they sit in the dark parlor in December, the family on chairs in a semicircle around the castiron stove, under high candles, working. The ox-cart man sews a harness. His wife and girl children sew, knit, spin, weave. His boys work with leather, carve, whittle. They work, and the years move on in paths and circles of work. From the dark underground of dead winter the year moves to woodchopping, ice cutting, deer hunting, tanning, coopering, sugaring, manuring, plowing, planting,

weeding, haying, harvesting, slaughtering, and filling the cart again, for the journey to Portsmouth.

I see that the ox-cart man is a perennial plant, divesting himself each year of everything grown, and growing it all again. When I dream his face I see Paul's face, who harvests a story for me, and I see my grandfather's face, who divested himself of everything he could gather, in his stewardship carrying all the past through winter darkness into present light. I understand: This duty is my duty also. If people like Wesley and Kate, like Paul and Bertha, not only live out their lives but pass on the stories of their lives — their own and the stories dead people told them — by these stories our seasons on earth may return and repeat themselves in others.

Let the curve of my story meet the curve of your own.

THE FIRE THAT
NEVER WENT
OUT

WELL, it *did* go out, in summer's heat when only noontime dinner need be cooked and supper was cold, or in spring or autumn when the night would be mild and the range's heat unnecessary. In the 1930s and the wartime 1940s, we let the fire die down when we went to bed at nine o'clock, and we thundered it up again, five the next morning, with a cup of kerosene flung over kindling. Only in winter, perhaps, did the fire never go out. December into early March, my grandfather in overalls carried armfuls of maple and ash from the woodshed to fill the woodbox fitted between range and papered wall. Then my grandmother, the kitchen's broad and powerful matriarch, tended the range's firebox, alternating kinds and cuts of wood according to need. When she required high heat in the oven, for bread and pies, ash blazed; midafternoon, various hardwoods steamed the kettle slowly, at the ready for coffee. At night, tight maple or elm heated slow and reliable.

In the morning — after oatmeal, pork scraps, and fried eggs, sometimes with potatoes hot or cold, always with bread and yesterday's leftover pie — the stove heated to assemble noontime's dinner: potatoes again, vegetables out of the blue Ball jars that lined shelves in the rootcellar, maybe boiled beef or fowl, roast mutton, pork. Baking once a week collected breads and pies to store in the milk room. Supper was dinner diminished, cold in summer, in winter supplemented with hot beans from the oven or pies warmed up.

At summer's end, in August and hot September, the prodigious canning took all day, week after week. It had begun early in the summer with peas; now it was Kentucky Wonders, corn sliced from the cob, pickled beets, tomatoes — a thousand jars every summer. Women's faces and bare arms stayed red for weeks, and in the rootcellar shelves bent under the tonnage of ripe summer alongside bins for the storage of roots and apples in autumn.

It is a Glenwood range, black and regularly blackened again. Dating from the first years of this century, it is ornamental like Victorian houses and furniture, its squat, elegant lines floral with castiron relief. The draft system — multiple sliding panels, doors and levers for internal alteration — allows both subtle control and decorative business. The oven door opens by hand, or if hands be occupied offers a foot pedal. Six lids lift from the stove's top, two over the small firebox, four gradually receding from the hottest places. But the whole large surface is for cooking and warming, with further warming shelves extending above the surface at the range's rear. Farthest from the firebox is the well or reservoir that kept water warm day and night — for filling the kettle, for lowering the aluminum dipper into when you needed hot water to wash and rinse the dishes — almost as easy as the hot-water faucet that takes its place. If quantities of hot water were needed, when the great washing machine with its fitted mangle was rolled in from the shed, kettles over the stove's whole surface heated gallons.

What an American creation, what a system, what a technology, this wonder mechanical, visible, and tangible, this mystery huge, heavy, and ornamental!

My mother remembers when the stove arrived in a great Railway Express wooden box carted by a team of horses. She remembers also finding under the Christmas tree the tiny replica Glenwood that I mentioned now rests in the back chamber.

When my grandfather died my grandmother was seventy-four,

and kept the stove going until she was almost ninety, splitting wood herself for many years, and using the good help of cousins. Then another technology fitted two kerosene burners into the old firebox and threaded slender pipes through walls to an oil drum outdoors near the old well. After several years of this luxury, one day the firebox split and exposed flame. My mother was visiting my grandmother then and wrote me a letter about it. She'd found a good secondhand white enamel kerosene-electric stove. The men who brought it were good enough to haul the old Glenwood off to the barn until somebody could be found to drag it to the Wilmot dump. I was not to feel too bad; there was no way it could be repaired.

But my daughter, who was eight years old, told stories about that range to friends back home, and when they were incredulous, she required me to photograph it. No one in the suburbs had ever seen anything so grand. So I telephoned, so I wrote a letter: *Please keep the stove in the barn. Please don't dump it.* Thus when I returned to live here myself, I found the Glenwood a sagging hulk that looked frail and tiny detached from its function and its kitchen dominion, turned red like November leaves, piled in the corner the barn made where it joined the grainshed. Down the road in Potter Place I discovered a man who worked with metal, Leslie Ford, a blacksmith who also pumped out cesspools and repaired small engines, a wiry craftsman snappy and waggish in his mid-sixties, who looked over the rust heap and thought probably he could do something about it.

Les kept the stove six months, complained bitterly about the task's difficulty, added firebrick to the firebox, improvised a grill from somebody's old coal stove, delivered and installed it in the kitchen, from which it had absented itself only five years in the last eighty, and charged too little. Now the Glenwood takes its place again, with its old dignity, squat and horizontal, festooned with pedals and knobs, with its weightiness both literal and figurative. Its reservoir leaks but a hot-water faucet supplies our needs. Its firebox is narrow but we keep the stove going twenty-four hours a day only in coldest weather, when its fire allows habitation of half downstairs and prevents the kitchen water pipes from freezing. When it is thirty below I wake every two hours to feed it. Otherwise in winter we fire it in the morning (with twisted newspaper, not with kerosene) and let it cool down after dinner, which assembles itself again on the Glenwood's black surface.

Where my grandmother fitted small skillets into the round holes over the naked fire, we set the wok's inverted dome; stew bubbles all day; soup rolls its knuckles of boil and froth — on the fire that seldom goes out.

THE EMBRACE
OF OLD AGE

WHEN I SPENT my summers here as a boy, my grandparents took me everywhere they went. We had no car. We didn't hitch up the horse to go to a drive-in movie, but we rode behind Riley to church on Sunday morning, and on Sunday night returned in the buggy for Christian Endeavor. We attended annual social events, in July the Church Fair and in August Old Home Day. Although my grandparents lived without anything that passes for entertainment in the 1990s — no car, no television, no VCR, no restaurants, no cocktail parties — they were remarkably cheerful. My grandfather especially had a fortunate temperament. He liked his work, and a little amusement went a long way. Occasionally we hitched up Riley for a special occasion: a family reunion, an auction, an eightieth birthday party, a funeral, a long-delayed visit to a dying cousin. When I was fourteen years old we went to Willard and Alice Buzzle's diamond wedding anniversary.

In preparation, my grandmother made three blueberry pies and a bagful of ginger snaps; my grandfather dusted the horse carriage, wiped off the harness, and curried Riley. Because the buggy's iron rims rattled on its wooden wheels — a dry August — we drove it across the railroad tracks to Eagle Pond and urged Riley against his better judgment to wade, pulling the carriage into shallow water. We sat there for a few minutes as I delighted in the strangeness, sitting still in the buggy in the pond's shallows while the wood swelled tight inside the rims. Then we drove back to the farm to dress and set out.

Willard and Alice were older than my grandparents, who were in their sixties. I remembered the Buzzles from Old Home Day: They were *old*. Alice had been seventeen when she was married, which made her ninety-two on her seventy-fifth wedding anniversary. Willard was exactly one hundred, married the day he turned twenty-five, which of course made today's celebration double. Diamond wedding anniversaries were rare enough; today we added a simultaneous one hundredth birthday party. Three weekly newspapers sent photographer-reporters to the Danbury Grange.

Horses and buggies were uncommon on the roads, though horse farmers were not unknown in 1943. The war kept traffic down, but a few dark square cars passed us on Route 4. My grandfather kept the buggy's right wheels on the shoulder, and I watched sand spin off the wheels like Fourth of July nightworks fountains. When we arrived at the Grange Hall, it was decorated red, white, and blue. As we alighted my grandfather spoke in Riley's ear and tied him loosely to a young maple, so that he could bend his neck to eat grass. Inside, the Grange walls were covered with photographs of past Grange presidents, and there was an American flag beside the stage in the front, the drawn curtain showing a view of Mount Kearsage painted by a local artist in 1906. We were early, of course, and so was everyone else. My grandmother cut her pies and set the pieces out on a long table covered with pies and cookies. Willard and Alice's sons Clarence and Frank scurried about, old men who moved with the sprightly energy of children anxious to please. Then a shout from the door told us that the bridal couple had arrived. I looked out to see Willard's Model A parked at the front door, driven by their surviving daughter Ada. Bride and bridegroom tottered up the steps, walking with canes held in outside hands so that they could join inside arms. They gripped each other fiercely, as if each were convinced that the other needed help. Willard looked the frailer as he climbed the Grange steps on his hundredth birthday and his seventy-fifth wedding anniversary, wavering over the worn wood stairs.

At the opened double doors Clarence and Frank took charge, each grasping one parent, and led them into the hall, where my grandmother at the organ belted out the Wedding March. Now the ancient small parents, on the arms of ancient small sons, with ancient daughter in the rear, walked slowly the length of the hall between the folding chairs set up for the ceremony, waving and acknowledging our waves like conquerors returned from the war that was not over. When Alice and Willard reached the end of the hall, my grandmother's fingers switched to "Happy Birthday." Everyone sang while a huge cake, big enough for everyone present, was wheeled into the crowd, topped with a hundred candles and the figurines of a bride and groom. Willard and Alice conspired with Ada, Clarence, and Frank to blow out the candles, taking many breaths, after a pause for a wish.

And I thought, What could they wish for? Not for a long life! Maybe for an easy winter? I studied Willard's infirmity. The skin of his hands was brown with liver spots, flesh hung like turkey wattles from his neck, and everything about him shook: his arms, his head on its frail stem, and his bony knees visibly trembling against his trouser legs. I felt horror — as if it were indecent to be alive with no future, each day merely a task for accomplishment. My vision of old age shook me as Willard shook.

Our minister, Kate's brother my uncle Luther, was host and master of ceremonies for half an hour of reminiscences and songs: "The Old Oaken Bucket," "When You and I Were Young, Maggie," "Down by the Old Mill Stream." Luther read two telegrams, one for the wedding and one for the birthday, from President Franklin Delano Roosevelt. When we broke to eat I heaped my paper plate with hermits and brownies and cherry pie, not forgetting a piece of wedding cake. Returning for seconds, I gathered the last piece of my grandmother's blueberry.

Then I was bored. I was rarely bored in my grandparents' company but today they paid me no mind. They had done introducing me and I had done with comments on how tall I was. Now they stood with other old people recollecting together. And I felt separate, separated especially because I understood that I was the *only one* in this crowd able to see clearly the futility and ugliness of old age.

So I prowled around the building, exploring the stage behind the painted curtain, finding a closet full of ancient costumes, trying on a top hat and derby. Then I opened a door I had not entered before, a green room to the side of the stage, and walked into the dimness without sensing the presence of others. In low light from a shaded window I saw two bodies embracing as they leaned against a wardrobe. I was embarrassed, I suppose because notions of embracing had begun to occupy me day and night. I started to back out, then saw that it was Willard and Alice who clung to each other, having crept from their thronged relatives and neighbors to this privacy. Their twin canes leaned on a box while their arms engaged each other. For a quick moment it was as if I saw, beyond the ancients in the green room, a young couple, seventy-five years back, who found a secret place to kiss and hug in.

Then I heard what she said: "Alice, Alice, Alice." She spoke urgently, "Alice, Alice," as if she were warning herself of something. At that moment I felt my grandfather's hand on my shoulder — it was time to go home; he had sought me out — and when I looked up I saw that he had heard. It was not until we were driving home that he mentioned it. I listened as he spoke — his voice controlled, as if he made a neutral observation, about the weather perhaps, that although the day was bright he wouldn't be surprised if it rained — saying, "Kate, Willard didn't know who Alice was."

TO WALK
A DOG

DOGS GIVE US an excuse for walking. They love us, we love them, and we walk them because it makes them happy.

Gus is a golden retriever–sheepdog cross, affectionate and agreeable, handsome and guilty, who presides over the walkable acreage of our hearts. Like most dogs Gus is an enthusiast, not least for perambulation. In our house as in many, when Jane and I plan out the day, we are reduced to spelling words out: w-a-l-k. For *us* it may be walking; for Gus it is running and halting, often combined in a cartoonish maneuver as Gus skids, stopping in mid-sprint, scattering gravel. His acute olfactory sensor has bleeped him information of irresistible fascination — some woodland creature, seldom encountered, has decorated a bush with its odor-iferous Kilroy: coyote, skunk, bear, moose, otter, badger, raccoon, beaver, fisher, fox . . . Who knows?

Gus cannot run loose, because our house sits beside a busy two-lane blacktop that killed my grandfather's dogs as early as the 1920s. Good walking, however, waits all about us. Our house sits like an egg in a nest of twenty dirt roads, from which old logging trails slant up-mountain. Often we walk Gus on New Canada Road, which lopes its cursive along the side of Ragged Mountain, up and down but mostly up in both directions. As we trudge New Canada, Gus flashes into the woods after a flickering chipmunk, disappears into hemlock or birch or ash, and then reappears fifty yards ahead, calmly sitting in the ditch to wait for us while we absurdly whistle for him into the dark shade where he vanished.

Watching him run is purest joy. I walk doggedly ahead while Gus loses himself in rapt contemplation of something about a stone that I lack equipment to contemplate. After five minutes of intense rhinal analysis, acute ecstasy of nose, while I have pumped ahead uphill puffing, Gus covers the distance in one eighth the time. I crave watching him. At the top of the hill, where I can see his whole trajectory, I whistle. Having catalogued five hundred items around the examined stone, he looks up and remembers me. He coils himself like a spring, flattens on the air, and breaks the all-world up-Ragged hundred-meter record — every afternoon, all over again.

While I trudge, or while I pause for him, my eyes perform like Gus's nose. On New Canada Road I can walk the same path, day after day, and every day uncover new glory of the Creation. Over the divided seasons I study stone walls, which used to keep sheep out of corn, as they extend into dense woods. I contemplate thick-waisted matronly birches, dark hemlocks, and every spring the fragile, indomitable ferns. Streams hurtle after spring rains and become dry stony gulches of August. Leaves fall, snow decorates, moss blossoms, and I walk each day through an anthology of natural growth, change, and stasis, pausing to stare at the same mossy granite that Gus pauses to inhale. Six legs walking provide pleasures for two grateful eyes and one lengthy learned nose.

*When you live as a free-lance writer in New Hampshire, when
you have been known to write about the land and the people, an
editor telephones asking you to write about New England seasons.
Two years later, the same editor wants you to write about New
England weather. When you suggest that maybe the weather and
the seasons are the same subject, the editor says, "Okay? A thousand words?" In two years perhaps you have undergone sufficient
new experience to write another essay. Then of course there are
particular moments, like October and snow.*

*To begin with, here's a small piece that looks like the précis of
a book I wrote later.*

THE
ONE THOUSAND
SEASONS

NEW YORK has people, the Northwest rain, Iowa soybeans, and
Texas money. New Hampshire has weather and seasons. Convention speaks merely of four seasons; here, we number at least
a thousand, and on one good day our spendthrift climate runs
through seven or eight. Robert Frost lived his first eleven years
in monoseasonal California; maybe that's why he became the
laureate of climatic mutability. In "Two Tramps in Mud Time,"
he wrote about an April day. For a warm moment you think it's
May; then with sudden wind and cloud, "you're two months back
in the middle of March."

October may be more so. When we wake, we stoke the Glenwood and scrape ice off the pickup's windshield; at noon we take lunch sitting on the porch in T-shirts; the spot of rain at teatime is cold enough to send us checking the salt supply in the grain-shed, but sunset blooms a soft rose in the west, promising Indian summer, a promise we remember with chagrin when we wake at midnight to the first snowfall.

However we number them, spring is the least of our seasons. It begins with the glorious disaster of winter's melt, periodic in March, interrupted by blizzards, continuing through April as rivers roll down hillsides where no rivers were, gullying tunnels under snowdrifts, hollowing gray scrap bulwarks as rag-and-tatter as snow in Manhattan. When snow goes, mud takes over. For a week or two we struggle in mud as we never struggled in snow. Transmissions bust, the pond road is travel-at-your-own-risk, the bridge is out, and Fred keeps revving up the tractor to haul flatlanders out of the ditch, the way Fred's grandfather Fred did with his oxen.

When mud goes dry, leaving stiff ridges and warps for bumping over, we do not sigh in relief, for if we sigh we inhale black-flies. We wish the mud back; it does not raise welts. Now snow-drops fly their small flags in our gardens, now daffodils rise in tentative glory — always, every year, the bravest rewarded with cupfuls of snow, in *Return of the Son of Winter*, rerun on every channel — but we do not wander happily on the daffodil hillside. We feel our joy behind windows, even storm windows, looking past the last garbage snow to the sun's blossoming hill — unless we are careless of skin or rapturous of bite and scratch. And when the blackflies go, perhaps the mosquitoes have eaten them.

But even the least of seasons is beautiful. As we drive to the store, or as we garden protected by thick socks and a beekeeper's mask, we move under the frail green of beginning leaves. There is nothing so tender as new green, smoke of red and yellow buds along with pale green smoke, loosening at the branch ends of trees released from the cold hold of winter. Whole hillsides over-night smolder up this tenderness, leaves unfolding daily and darkening week by week toward the vigorous black-green of sum-mer's oak and maple. Now we walk, our hands slapping the air as if we bargained for a thousand rugs in a thousand Turkish

markets, and inspect the winter's waste by pond and mountain-
side: what popples the beaver took, what birches we lost to February's icestorm.

If spring is least it is also shortest. There are those who claim
it occupies only the month of May. (Some few insist that spring
occurs on May 17, ten A.M. to two-thirty P.M.) But unless we confront a literalist of the calendar, there can be no controversy over
the date of summer's beginning. The rest of us plant our gardens,
except for the peas we scatter on snow, after the full moon closest
to Memorial Day — but the summer people seed themselves on
Memorial Day itself. All summer as corn inches up or doesn't,
as the zucchini population of New Hampshire multiplies like
Nashua, as green tomatoes wax and decide with heroic stubborn-
ness to remain forever green, the growth of summer people outdoes every other crop. Through drought and deluge, unseason-
able cold or Bostonian mug and swelter, they pop from the
cracked earth of June by the hundred thousand; they spread in
July up, out, and over the rural dirt of New England; they take
into themselves abundancies of sun and water; they thrive, fat-
ten, elongate, swell, ripen — only, on Labor Day, afflicted suddenly by minus three hundred degrees of school-frost, work-frost,
and duty-frost, instantly to wither, blacken, die, and vanish.

On their sudden, seasonal, and predictable disappearance — we
hear of them miraculously altered, no longer tanned in the flesh
but brown-suited in worsted as in Worcester, and felt-hatted in
the suburbs of the ordinary life — we sigh without inhaling a
single insect, enjoy the huge dark end-of-summer leaves, tidy our
spent gardens, and hunker down for the best of times. The red
branch on the green tree starts it off, one eruption marching to a
different drummer. Then whole bogs blaze with swamp maples,
dear deep reds followed by the great vulgar chorus of bellowing,
billowing yellows, reds, russets, and rusts. Birch, maple, rare
elm, oak, beech, ash, each in its own time and with its own pitch
and tone swells the outlandish chorus. It is the London Phil-
harmonic tripling up with orchestras from Bogotá and Kuala
Lumpur, Spike Jones conducting, and each shade and position
contributes another violin, oboe, or triangle to the gorgeous ca-
cophony of autumn.

Always the persistent evergreen supplies the continuo. As autumn endures and the leaves fall, the silvery sheen of empty trunks and branches becomes an increasing theme. Everywhere we walk we gaze at yellow leaves against unpainted barns, towering enormous flame-fountains beside white houses, varicolored Kearsarge altering each day, and through the day, by variety of light. Best of all, we love the hills of middle distance, with color patches distinct when we focus on them; when we refocus on the whole hill, its colors contract to a single insane tweed of pinks, oranges, reds, russets, and silvers.

After the sober and noble palette of late October and November, analytic cubism with its rectangles of granite and released stone walls, New England's seasonal journey retracts to the oneness of winter, from outrageous multiplicity to white uniformity. Usually it begins at night, the black sky flaking full with whiteness, covering brown hayfield and granite hill, boulder, road, and barn with the soft silence of its frigidity. We gather inside around the noisy Glenwood; we gather ourselves inside ourselves for the three months of our annual descent, internal Persephones of the personal underworld. On the full moon's winter night pewtery light reflects upward from snow to flicker against tin ceilings, ghost light, and we howl like coy-dogs in the moon's light.

Of the one thousand seasons, winter by actual count provides four hundred and twenty-seven. Sixty-eight percent of winter's seasons cause pain. This pain's bright side is our complaining and bragging: Winter is ours, although winter people wearing skiing uniforms brighten white slopes. This long winter gives us our identity. Mixed and intense, beauty and pain together, interrupted only by January's thaw with its anticipatory melt — Miami invading from the South — winter is the name of our place. We must admit, spring is annoying, summer is not ours, autumn is best — and winter is New England's truest weather.

GOOD USE FOR
BAD WEATHER

My GRANDPARENTS nailed two thermometers side by side on the porch of their New Hampshire farmhouse. One registered ten degrees cold, the other ten degrees hot, so that there was always something to brag about. Every morning when my grandmother sat in the rocker under Christopher the canary, writing three postcards to three daughters, she could say, "Thirty below this morning. Seems like it might get cold." Or, "Ninety already and the sun's not over the mountain."

In New England we take pride in our weather because it provides us with pain and suffering, necessities for the spirit, like food and clothing for the body. We never brag about good weather. Let Tucson display self-esteem over eighty-three days without rain. Let Sarasota newspapers go free for the asking when the sun doesn't shine. We smirk in the murk, superior. It's true that we have good weather; we just don't pay it any mind. When summer people flock north to the lakes and the mountains, they do not gather to enjoy our foggy rain. If they're from Boston, they don't come *for* bright sun and cool dry air; they migrate north *against* the soup-kettle mugginess of home. It seems more decent.

In good weather — apple days of October, brilliant noons and cool evenings of August — we remain comfortable despite our pleasure by talking about pleasure's brevity, forecasting what we're in for as soon as the good spell is done with. Winter is best for bragging. For a week or two in March, mud is almost as good. (Mud is weather as much as snow is; leaves are landscape.) "Tried to get the Buick up New Canada this morning. Have to wait for a dry spell to pull it out, I suppose. Of course, we'll have to dig to find it, first."

Black ice is first rate, but most of us who cherish difficulty will settle for a good ten feet of snow. We get up about five-fifteen, make the coffee, check the thermometer: ten degrees above. The warmth must account for the snow. Highway department plows blunder down Route 4 in the dark outside. We get dressed, dragging on flannel-lined chinos, flannel shirt, sweater, down jacket, and boots. Then we broom one car, headlights and taillights, gun it in reverse over the hump of snow Forrest's plow left, swing it up Forrest's alley, and swoop it down to the road, scattering ridges of snow.

Only two miles to the store. It's not adventurous driving, but it pays to be attentive, to start slowing for a turn a hundred yards early. The store opens at six. Because this is New Hampshire, somebody's bound to be there by five-forty-five. We park with the motor running and the heater on — it'll get warm while we pick up the *Globe* — to go inside. Bob's there with his cup of coffee, and Bill who owns garage and store, and Judy the manager who makes coffee and change. We grin at each other as I stamp my boots and slip my paper out of the pile. We say things like, "Nice weather!" "Bit of snow out there!" "Hear we're getting two feet more!" but what we're really saying is *It takes more than a couple of feet of snow to slow us down!*

Weather is conversation's eternal subject, lingua franca shared by every New Englander with sensory equipment. When Rolls-Royce meets junker, over to the dump, they can talk about the damned rain. Weather talk helps us over difficult subjects. On one Monday morning some years ago, Ned said to Will, "Too bad about Pearl Harbor. I hear there's ten feet over on Five-A." Will said to Ned, "I suppose we'll lick 'em. They say a bread truck got through."

In a boring patch when the weather's mild, we talk about disasters and catastrophes of the past. As a child I heard endless stories about the Blizzard of '88. My Connecticut grandfather belonged to a club that met once a year on the anniversary to swap reminiscences — by which, of course, we understand that they met to tell lies. As I stagger into codgerhood, I discover that my own Blizzard of '88 is the great wind of 1938. I was in Connecticut for that one, which first visited our house in my father's disgust over his new barometer. He won it in a putting contest, and he was proud of it, pretty in its rich brown wood and bright brass. Then when he hung it on the wall it busted; at least it sank way, way down until the foolish thing predicted hurricane.

Most of the time, weather is relative. Every year when an August morning is forty degrees, we shiver and chill: It's *cold* out there! But when a February morning rises to forty, we walk around with our coats unbuttoned, enjoying the heat wave. Next day an icestorm, and we take relief in the return of suffering. It's true — if you don't have to drive in it — that there are few things in Creation as beautiful as an icestorm. Much bad weather is beautiful: dark days when it never quite rains and never quite doesn't, English weather cozy around the fire; wild rains of summer after high heat, compensation and relief; drizzle in autumn that drains color from the trees, quiet and private; the first snow, which steps my heartbeat up; the first *big* snow, which steps it higher; winter thaw, with its hesitant promise; gothic thunderstorms with bolts of melodrama — we quicken, we thrill, we comfort the dog.

Every now and then we have an open winter, as we call it when we have no snow; it's psychic disaster. It's disaster also for shrubs and bulbs, but it's the soul's woe because we haven't suffered enough. The earth can't emerge because it never submerged. We don't deserve the milder air and the daffodils rising because we haven't lost our annual battles with the snow — fender benders, bad backs from shoveling the mailbox, rasp of frozen air in the lungs, falls on ice, chunks of snow down our boots. The only bad weather in New England is when we don't have any.

OCTOBER'S
OMENS

EVERYWHERE in the north, October is gorgeous and ominous. Red omens of the maple tree, firing wild flares into the soft early twilight, prophesy white frozen winter, zero of January and February's drifts, blocked turnpikes and the wretched gutter-snow of the city. In New Hampshire the warnings begin early. Even August flies winter's sign in its red branch; frost visits in hesitant September. But in October, auspices of winter show themselves as steadily as the onset of a head cold, a tightening behind the eyes and a tentative sniffle. Up early to drive for the paper, we scrape omens from the windshield of the car. On the same frosty morning late hollyhocks sag blown brown rotten trumpets from spindly stalks. But noon warms up, October's message relents, and chrysanthemums and asters will endure — for a few weeks.

At this time of year, the vegetable gardener undergoes the fear of frost. If one day we read in the paper that the first deep cold is on its way, our tomato vines always hang a hundred great green globes. We pull old sheets from the back of the linen closet, and blankets with holes in them, to drape our plants against frost's killing scythe. Usually we ignore widespread pumpkins and squash, because the gourd will survive though the vine shrivel; if the zucchini expire we will feel only gratitude.

All night under the clear cold sky, starlight reflects from the ghostly white-sheeted tomato plants. Come anxious morning, we inspect the rows for green or brown; in lucky years our refrigerator-cold green tomatoes have survived. And if we endure a three-day flurry of early frost-fright, September or October, then maybe the sky will cloud up, ether will densen and warm . . . and Indian summer, lazing down Route 4, will redden the great globes of our tomatoes well into autumn — fresh red slices for sandwiches at lunch, beefsteaks and Better Girls for stewing up with onions at supper or for freezing toward the summery spaghettis of January.

If the vines die with hundreds of green tomatoes on them, the next morning we will rip up the tomato plants and hang them upside down in the cellar to ripen, or maybe we will pile green tomatoes in the shed wrapped in newspaper, or . . . There are as many solutions to the Problem of the Green Tomato as there are cures for hiccups. But it is a rule of October: No tomato picked green, however much it reddens in the afterlife of shed or root-cellar, will ever taste like a ripe tomato.

Frost-fears get us moving. It is time to check out the radiator coolant in the Saab, which overheated all summer, and test it for forty below; it is time to change plugs and points in the Datsun pickup, which retains old-style rear-wheel drive, so that we must examine the treads on snow tires. For many of us in New Hampshire, it is time to get the plow ready for bolting on to the V-8 four-wheel-drive truck; it is provident to grease up the snow-blower, not to mention the snowmachine. It is time for everyone of a northern persuasion to switch wardrobes, to air the mothball smell out of a drawerful of sweaters, to stash the light khakis of summer and recover L. L. Bean's flannel-lined jeans from the shelf at the back of the closet. Blazer and light flannel climb attic stairs as tweed and whipcord descend. Summer's sandals pack themselves away. We clear spider webs out of felt-lined boots and set them under the closet's down jacket.

In New Hampshire we measure the year by the category of flat-lander that the season elicits. When the leafers of autumn depart in mid-October, we know what we are in for. Deer hunters come in two formats: The local sort lives in a trailer down the road on Route 4, freezer packed with deer meat against a layoff at the shoe factory; the other sort drives up from Massachusetts, paunchy Rambo geared with red vest and cap, geared with .30-30 and Four Roses. When he hunts he is drunk by seven A.M., and every autumn he shoots two or three laid-off shoemakers trying to stock their freezers.

For this reason, among others, the two formats do not get along. Flatlander feels that countryman lacks the sporting sense; New Hampshire doubts Rambo's ability to distinguish a deer's track from a chipmunk's, or even a railroad's. My favorite sign of autumn was handwritten, irregular, indignant block capitals two feet high on a bedsheet stapled to a fence in Vermont. I saw it last November, just after deer season: THIS IS A DONKEY!

In October everybody in the northern half of the country prepares to heat houses. We check our furnaces, gas or oil or propane; if we heat by wood, we stack split logs — eight cord for the winter, maybe — and if we are sensible we clean the chimney. Then we hunker down. Everywhere winter approaches by its own weird routes. In northern Michigan and in Canada provident people test the electrical systems that, plugged in all night, keep their cars warm enough to start. In Florida they check out the smudge pots. I don't know *what* they do in Arizona. In California people look at the grass, hoping it may turn green this year, and if it does, and the rains keep coming, people watch in terror for the mountainous Godzilla of a mud slide ingesting Jacuzzi, carport, deck, and conversation pit. In West Texas, old desert reclaimed for cotton by irrigation and diminishing aquifer, people watch with irritation and annoyance as the single tree next to the house in the country drops brown leaves, littering the precious patch of lawn. Every year outside Lubbock a homeowner, outraged by the sheer mess of falling leaves, rents a chainsaw from Taylor's and saws down the old live oak that was planted and nursed, fifty years ago, by someone homesick for northeastern elms.

Here in New Hampshire, we would need to hire the province of Quebec to clear-cut the entire state if we wanted to prevent leaves from messing up our yards. Unwilling to undertake such a project, and putting a good face on things, we use our leaves. In November, maybe during deer season when we cannot walk in the woods, it is time to tuck up the house. Nowadays some of us are insulated, and the old house is tight, but tightness is not a property traditional among country houses, where icy winds at floorboard level riffle the braided rugs. To cut down on the breeze that blows through the clapboard, we rake maple leaves (oak, ash, anything) against the foundation stones of the house high onto clapboard. To keep the piles in place we cut hemlock branches, green on red, and lay them across the leaves. When the first snow comes we shovel it over the leaves and against the house, best insulation of all, and all winter when a thaw melts snow back from the wood, we shovel new snow into the cold gap. (Naturally all this damp rots clapboard; we need to replace boards every fifty years or so.) Often we tack poly around the base of the house before we pull leaves against it. We buy it down to the lumberyard in great rolls and wrap up the house with it, rural Christos, tacking it three feet high. Some folks prefer black tarpaper, some Reynolds Wrap. Houses on Route 4 sport extra socks and leggings like arctic explorers.

By October's end or early November we have checked out the heating, winterized the car, tucked up the house, switched clothing, and pulled up the garden. Now we are permitted to wait. One night we will wake conscious of a soft advent, quietness dropping from the air; we will gaze into darkness to watch the great white onset of winter. We will rise in the morning, virtue's reward, in a warm house to don warm clothing, and to start a car that will start. The most foresighted among us will even have stationed snow shovels and pails of salt by the kitchen door. *Sigh* . . . It helps to remember that winter is ominous of spring.

A GOOD FOOT
OF SNOW

CHRISTMAS DAY, snow started before dawn. In the blackness of five A.M. we heard the snowplows rumble north and rumble south, shaking the oak sills of our farmhouse, comforting us in our beds. All winter plows made cold thunder: up . . . down . . . up . . . down. Sometimes the vibration wakes us, and we roll over, under heaped blankets, snugly aware of where we are. Sometimes I rise, add wood to the fires banked in our castiron stoves, flip on the porch light to see our driveway's accumulation, and wait for the plow to turn and return. In the distance, like a freight train thirty years ago, the grunt and shudder begins; then the bright headlights illuminate snow; then, in a tidal wave of thrust whiteness, great Hokusai coils of dazzle fly gutterwards, almost hiding the dark body of the truck; and in the upward light snow falls as thick as cloth.

Christmas Day at five A.M., the plow's shudder waked six-year-olds up and down Route 4, to stretch and remember suddenly what *day* it was, to turn on a bedroom light and look for a full stocking. And the sea captains of the snow, great plowers over the road, never reached home until nighttime — cold turkey and stuffing among crabby children, toys already broken — for the snow kept up all day until night returned at five in the afternoon. All day the party lines trilled up and down the countryside, distant relatives deciding to postpone long trips, close brothers and sisters reassuring each other that the roads were fine, driveways dug out. All day the bright sky flaked white against the dark pine climbing Ragged Mountain behind us. All Christmas Day the snow mounted on barn roof, birdfeeder, and useless mailbox. All day we gazed at the white world. By nightfall the radio told us: We had accumulated eighteen inches of snow.

Snow turns us back two hundred years. When the plow disappears down the road, the road sinks out of sight between the whiteness of ditches and fields. Bright stillness thick with flakes hovers on tree and barn, hill, pond, and meadow. I stand in the white doorway, in front of the still house, squinting to take the country back before highways, trains, and snowplows.

Then a pickup crushes ahead over the plowed Route 4, carrying someone home for Christmas.

All Christmas Day we looked for Forrest to come and plow us out. My big cousin, contractor and carpenter and winter plowman, plows the parking lot at the ski slope on Ragged as well as numerous private driveways. At noon his pickup burst up one side of our U-shaped driveway and pushed the snow back once-over-lightly behind our cars; if we needed to go someplace, we could shovel a minute, back out, and swoop to the road. All day we waited for him to return, for the fifteen minutes of backing and charging that clears all portions of our driveway, pushes snow back onto leachfield and daffodil patch, up to woodshed and car-

riage shed. Sometimes when we've had thirty or forty inches without a melt, Forrest will hire a front loader to heap drift on drift, farther out into roses and asparagus, clearing space for the next accumulation. Although Forrest complains about cold and no sleep and long hours, I never see him so happy as when he is perched high over his blade — backing, gathering speed, changing the blade's tilt, and *whomp* into the plain of whiteness, shoving it around like a large child in the best sandbox.

It was pitch black early Christmas night, and we were ready for bed, when the sound of Forrest's plow came through to us, and high in the black yard gleamed the yellow eye of his truck's forehead. Back and *whomp*. Back and *whomp*. We watched him skillfully shift and back and thud and thud, with the grace of an ocean liner, of a 747, of a seven-foot tight end — anything huge and doing well what it loves to do. Forrest slammed into our eighteen inches, Forrest tucked it, Forrest treated it like a flurry.

Half done, he parked and paused, as he often does. Water boiled on the wood stove, and Forrest accepted the offer of a cup of coffee. And when he came in, his beard whitened, his eyes red, smiling and shaking his head, we heard him say, "Yes, that's a good foot." He paused for emphasis, repeated, "A *good* foot of snow."

There's more to New Hampshire than Eagle Pond.
 Dick Ketchum, of Blair & Ketchum's Country Journal, *pointed
me in the direction of Heman Chase, for which I remain grateful.
Heman died two years ago at eighty-six.*

HEMAN CHASE'S
CORNERS

ONE DAY in August of 1983 I went surveying with Heman
Chase, who has been measuring land in Vermont and New Hampshire since 1928. In order to start first thing in the morning, I
stayed overnight in the house that Heman and Edith built in
1936, in the town of East Alstead, New Hampshire, where Heman
has spent most of his many-sided life. Being a surveyor is only
Heman's vocation; by avocation he writes books, runs a water-
mill, invents useful devices, philosophizes, and uncovers local
history.

Surveying was the morning's task. After breakfast we descended to the under-house garage, where Heman keeps the truck
he uses for surveying. His Bronco is twelve years old, with eighty-
seven thousand miles on it. And this Bronco has a lot on it besides miles. Heman has equipped it as ingeniously as the British
secret service outfits a sports car for James Bond. A clock, an al-
timeter, and a pencil sharpener are screwed to the dashboard. At
the front of the hood he has fixed an antique bell from Manches-

ter, Vermont, bartered from a dealer for whom Heman felled an elm. On the front bumper Heman has attached a telescoping device for pushing cars without doing damage to pusher or pushee. As he shows me how it works, Heman remembers a story. In 1928 his Model T got stuck in a snowstorm at Craig's Four Corners; he slogged uphill to Ike Craig's farmhouse, and Ike Craig hitched up his oxen to a logging chain to pull him out. When Heman tried to pay him, Ike waved him off. "Pass it on," said Ike Craig, and Heman has been passing it on ever since.

Surveying equipment fills the Bronco's truck bed. It will be a warm day, and Heman wears a tank top over his wiry chest and shoulders, heavy trousers against the brush, and old sneakers for his work in the woods. Today Heman says that he will use compasses, to save the client time and money. Machines that measure more precisely are expensive and time-consuming. "We are always being pushed to be more technological," Heman begins; he has arrived at a favorite subject. "A compass survey is accurate within one in three hundred and fifty or so, adequate where we're going. People who spend their time in an easy chair in an office now say we ought to get it one in five thousand." Heman snorts, and seems to change the subject by referring to old-fashioned telephone operations. "Back when Mrs. Buzzle was Central, once I tried to get Mr. Marsh the minister. Mrs. Buzzle said, 'You'd better wait five minutes, he just walked past the window.' "

Heman looks over to see if I get the point; he had not changed the subject. "Maybe all this homogeneity," he says, "leaves us free to read poetry and do inward things." He is being ironical. It is not that Heman dislikes machines. In fact, he has invented many useful devices. As we get ready to back out of the garage, I observe a Chase invention: Heman pushes lightly against the garage door and it lifts up easily, its weight balanced by an egg-shaped stone fixed to the end of a twelve-foot wooden spoke. When the door is open, its granite counterweight poises in air like a dinosaur's egg over a cave mouth.

As we drive to Alstead Center, Heman discusses the appropriate technology of surveying, in his crisp, deliberate voice. He parks on a wood road by the parcel of land we will survey for possible subdividing and selling. Heman opens drawers and panels in the Bronco's back end — as compartmentalized as a Swiss army knife — and removes some tools of the trade: a compass on a tripod, a hundred-foot spool of metal surveyor's tape, a red-and-white-striped pole for sighting through the compass, a machete, and bug spray.

Now Hallie Whitcomb arrives, Heman's co-worker, a slim woman in her late twenties, strong, shy, friendly, giving off senses of both farm girl and intellectual. On his stationery Heman lists Hallie as his assistant. When he first told me about her, he spoke of Hallie as if she were a miracle. Six years back she dropped over, a total stranger *out of the blue*, to visit Heman and Edith. She had grown up on a farm in Springfield, Vermont, where she still lives, and had studied geologic mapping at Earlham College in Indiana; she thought she would like to try surveying for a while. After the visit Edith told Heman, "Give her a chance." Heman gave her a chance. "I call her a partner now," he says. "She just about as often tells *me* what to do as I tell *her* what to do." About one social matter Heman feels especially grateful. "I'm glad that I lived into an age — or *to* an age — such that it's not considered improper for her to work with me."

Heman has already explained the morning's task: We will follow the old backline through eight hundred feet of forest, and set a new corner for the putative subdivision. Heman leads the way. We set off for the place we will start from. We head into the woods; the woods take us over: up precipitous banks slippery with pine needles, down steep sides to streams layered with flat round stones as black as slate. We clutch at saplings; we dig our fists into cliff faces of needles. Our leader in his tank top wields his machete rapidly, cuts off sharp dead hemlock boughs with a quick powerful wrist stroke — intrepid, single-minded, and overheated.

A great hemlock marks the corner from which we begin to measure. Heman nails on the tree's trunk a metal plate that bears his name, the initials of the owner, and the date. From this tree we set out, Heman leading with his barber pole in one hand and his brush-cutting machete in the other, slashing blazes on trees on either side of his path, progressing at north fifty-four degrees west. Hallie takes up the rear with compass and tripod. When Heman has traveled eighty or ninety feet ahead, still visible, he stops for Hallie to check the line. She sights Heman's barber pole in the open sights of the compass, and tells him to move a foot to the right, or six inches to the left. With his own hand-held compass Heman counterchecks the reading; if his compass differs, he moves to split the difference. The tape counts the distance traveled, and Hallie keeps track.

Sometimes I forge ahead with Heman, sometimes stay behind with Hallie. As I scramble up and down, following our bearing down gullies and up hills, I lose my reading glasses from my shirt pocket. This loss annoys me, because I was foolish to bring my reading glasses into the woods. Heman stops what he is doing and crawls around on his hands and knees searching for my glasses. "What color are they?" says Heman, and I tell him that the rims are gold. "Well," he says drily, "if I find any silver ones I won't pick them up." I think of how, in fifty years, someone surveying these woods again — or digging in a suburban garden, or starved and scrabbling for a root to eat — will discover a pair of old-fashioned glasses deep in leaf mold.

Finally I persuade Heman to return to the attack, and I talk with Hallie as he marches forward, carrying his skinny pole before him like a relay racer with a six-foot baton. At the family farm in Springfield Hallie keeps a big garden, she tells me, and surveying is a good job for her. She works no more than half-time, three or four days a week, nine months a year; she wants only as much money as she needs. She loves surveying, loves Heman, approves of using the compass. "He keeps the client in mind," says Hallie. "Land values are rising, though. . . . We may have to be more precise." Maybe it's not only people in office easy chairs who want Heman to measure one in five thousand.

As we talk, we keep moving. Ninety feet and eighty-seven and ninety-four. We are two hundred and seventy-one feet toward our eight-hundred-foot goal, where we will make a corner and head for the road. Heman draws a line through trackless wood that was pasture once. This land was never cultivated. There are too many stones for that, granite and quartz, and there is no feel underfoot of ridges that a plow made. Its pasture days are a long way back, maybe fifty years, maybe a hundred. Old trees with trunks two feet thick have given up the ghost and lie across our path. Sharp branches scrape our skin. Though Heman hacks a gap, it is a Heman-sized gap, for a body smaller and suppler than mine.

Everywhere the prolix morbidity of the natural world has toppled old trees to the ground and started new ones up. No atom of space is unoccupied, by infant or by corpse, by needle or moss or tiny purple flower. Young trees stretch out in a row, pushed over by one gust; old trees root deep to endure. One hardy birch grips its root into earth around a round hunk of quartz the way a six-fingered pitcher might grasp a baseball. Everywhere among roots and in mosses there are holes for snake, mink, rabbit, skunk, and bigger holes for woodchuck. We find the droppings of deer and fox, yet nowhere do we see an animal; insects and the birds who eat them fly around us, but nothing larger shows itself.

Through it all — hacking, indomitable — Heman Chase draws a mapmaker's line, making a human mark on the vital, mori- bund, unstoppable energy and decay of the natural world. He draws a line through the wilderness, order imposed on chaos, the way a railroad draws a line through valley and forest, over stream and past meadow. I remember something Heman told me earlier, about a day when he and Hallie were setting a line. Deep in the woods, in bypassed rural New Hampshire, the old man and young woman found a stone culvert supporting aban- doned railroad track, and marveled at the beauty of its construc- tion: "Cut granite stones about three feet by a foot and a half, laid up without mortar in an arch to support a deep fill, a hun- dred feet through." Marveling, they ate lunch together in the woods, Heman a sandwich, Hallie "some vegetable concoction." In summary, Heman tells me, "We go around and find out what history was."

When Heman draws a mapmaker's approximate line through the moral wilderness, he does it by anecdote and by reference to his secular saints. The night before the survey, under trees near his house over Warren's Pond, he spoke about some of his professors at the University of Wisconsin. (He likes to say that his father thought Harvard the only place, his stepfather thought MIT the only place, and his mother packed him off to Wisconsin.) Professor Louis Kahlenberg was a moral example, an outstanding scientist who was forced to teach freshman chemistry — to the benefit of the freshmen — because he refused to work on chemical warfare during the First World War. Of course, a teacher can provide a counterexample. Another engineering professor, to whom Heman mentioned that he would take a philosophy course, observed, "All right, but it won't get you ahead."

For Heman the greatest ethical model is Henry George, the American economist and author of *Progress and Poverty*, who proposed a single tax on land. In Heman's first book, *American Ideals*, he connected George's idea with the society envisioned by this nation's founders. With land the ultimate determiner of wealth and power, George saw the concentration of land ownership as the greatest source of inequality and inequity in the world. If a land tax were our only means of revenue, then no one could aggregate masses of land and everyone could share in it — a democracy of small landowners. "George was the man who, more than any other, understood how the earth would have to be shared."

But Henry George's ideas do not find general acceptance among economists. One time Heman picked up a hitchhiking college student who majored in economics at Middlebury College in Vermont. Naturally enough, Heman asked his guest what he had learned in his classes about Henry George. The senior graduating in economics had never heard the name. Back home, after simmering down, Heman wrote a letter to the chairman of the economics department at Middlebury, offering his services as an unpaid lecturer on Henry George. After a long delay he was invited to address a class, and he enjoyed his visit to Middlebury, which ended in a long discussion with students who adjourned to the house of a history professor. Early on, however, Heman lost the class's economics teacher. He emphasized that under George's scheme there would be no income tax at all, and the professor, looking incredulous, asked, "Not even for Ted Williams?" Now, Heman's interests were wide-ranging but not universal: He didn't know who Ted Williams was. From the tone of the question, Williams was obviously an important figure. In the recesses of his mind Heman suddenly recollected that Ted Williams belonged to the sporting world. Figuring that his ignorance would undermine his advocacy, he merely affirmed, "Not even for Ted Williams." The professor of economics allowed that he could not countenance any tax scheme that refused to tax an income of a *hundred thousand dollars.*

Supper done, we walked back to the house carrying trays. Heman always walks tilted slightly forward, as if he were trudging uphill. Or he leans like the tower at Pisa, as tough as Pisan stone, with abrupt angular energy. He speaks little of age. Sometimes he remembers that he is old — as if with surprise. Back in the house he told a story about a lawsuit in 1940, when he had been hired to map a crossroads where a young man and an old had collided automobiles. The young man sued and lost, but that was not the point of the story. When the young man testified he was asked his age, and he replied brightly, as if he were proclaiming virtue, "Twenty-seven!" When the old man took the stand he was asked the same question. As Heman mimicked his answer, the old man pronounced his years with a mixture of tones: bemusement, bewilderment, recognition that it did not matter, amazement that he should have lived so long. He said in a lingering voice, "Seventy-seven." As Heman told the story, he too was seventy-seven.

Before bed we visited Chase's Mill. One of Heman's books, *Short History of Mill Hollow*, tells the story of the various water-power mills that used Mill Brook or Warren Brook, flowing out of Warren's Pond. It is a remarkable essay, combining archaeological detective work with a spirited defense of water power. Now we visited the actual place, where hundreds of children and adults have learned the old ways of water power. Chase's Mill is a large building topped by a great loft with a fireplace, site of community gatherings. Outside, set into the ground, is an enormous gristmill stone from an earlier mill. On the ground floor above the mill's works is the shop, with water-powered lumber planer, large table saw, and jointer, together with electric-powered drill presses, band saw, table saw, wood lathe, machinist's lathe, and emery wheels. Here Heman and Edith have held shop classes for local children, teaching them to work in wood and metal.

As we entered the shop in August, I noticed a large wood stove back against a wall, out of the way. Heman showed how the castiron body pivots on skids into the room's center for the winter cold, its stovepipe artfully jointed to pivot in agreement. The shop is equipped to manufacture whatever ingenuity requires. Here Heman has implemented inventions: tripods for surveying, his own screw for splitting cord wood; he has made Windsor footstools and dumpcart bodies, trestle tables, cradles, and coffins for his mother and stepfather.

Heman stepped excitedly over the busy floor, pointing out, explaining; I realized that Heman is one of nature's professors, a doer who enjoys professing what he does. Although I am ignorant of mechanics and machines, enthusiasm pulled me in. I found myself watching intently as Heman cut a zigzag piece of brass, polished, trimmed . . . Then we descended to the floor beneath, and moved inward toward the source of the old mill's power. The walls were rough stone, and I heard water dripping. Plunging in front of us, a nineteen-inch iron perstock channeled water to a turbine two stories down. At the moment the mill was quiet: alert, suspended, waiting. Lower down, at midlevel, we walked in a maze of pulleys, belts, and shafting now silent as the works of a huge abandoned clock.

Then Heman pulled a lever: CRASH, and a hurtle of water deafened us as inside these deep, narrow chambers a liquid column smashed into the turbine, urging it into spinning life. All over the mill wheels whirled, cogs spun, gears groaned interlocking, long belts turned their quarter turns. An immense intricacy of mechanic power, loosed by Heman's hand on a lever, resurged the power of the clockmaker-engineer; we lived inside a clock of power, shaking, whirling with the force of twenty tumultuous horses straining to pull, smoothly and steadily, a system, a church, a cave, the thunderous center of the earth. And as Heman saw its effect, he grinned like a boy.

We descended toward the tumult of water. Heman recounted, shouting, a sequence of sluices: an old wooden one, an iron one that he rescued from an abandoned mill, this new one only seven years old. Then he pointed to another pipe, a second, smaller sluice, as if the big one had dropped a foal, which connected to a tiny version of the big turbine. Over the small sluice was a hand lever that Heman asked me to pull. When I did, water spun into the small turbine, from which a wire moved upward to a little machine on a level above. The little machine was a car's generator, and over it Heman had hung an electric light. As the small turbine spun it generated electricity; slowly, flickering at first, a light bulb illuminated the deep hollow of Chase's Mill.

Heman offered congratulations: "You just lit a light by hydro-electric power!"

Now in the woods, surveying, we have come eight hundred feet, and it is time to make a corner. First we gather rocks, mostly lumps of granite from football size to the size of a basketball. To pry out medium stones, Heman wedges his machete under them. For larger rocks he takes a stick of hemlock, sharpens the end, uses another stone as a fulcrum, and lifts the rock out to roll it toward the pile. In twenty minutes we have collected a small quarry. Then Heman inserts a stout hemlock stake in the middle of the rock pile, big stones at the bottom showing their moss, smaller stones wedged closer in. Taking another metal patch from his pocket, he pokes his initials onto it and the date of this day and this year when we set out this line and made this corner.

Then we all stand back to look at it — a cairn of stones embodying purpose, a stick with a metal tag announcing a deed — and I feel for a moment as if I had taken part in a ritual, partly because this device resembles a grave. Out of the silence Heman's voice declares this sign a sacrament, and Hallie adds:

"Nobody makes a corner like Heman Chase."

New England Monthly, *in its early years noted for its asperity,*
solicited from me an essay that would explain why New Hamp-
shire people loathed Vermont. I was delighted to comply. At the
same time, as the editors told me, they were soliciting a parallel
piece — why Vermont hates New Hampshire — from my friend
Richard Ketchum, who co-founded B & K's Country Journal. *Dick*
Ketchum is a kindly sort, and I should have been prepared. While
I composed this jeremiad, Ketchum wrote an essay gently favor-
ing Vermont, in which a few paragraphs mildly suggested that
perhaps New Hampshire wasn't quite so nice *as Vermont was.*
When the paired essays appeared, in 1986, I was revealed as a
curmudgeon and my essay, which had been solicited as "Why I
Hate Vermont," appeared under the title "Why I Love New
Hampshire."

REASONS FOR
HATING VERMONT

VERMONTERS lead quiet, introspective lives among the un-
spoiled splendors of their countryside, interrupted only by
brunches, cocktail parties, and *Masterpiece Theatre*. Vermont
invented the Young Rural Professional in 1972; in the same year,
the yrppie invented Vermont. But it is not true that Vermonters
live a serene existence without worries of any kind. The editor
of a distinguished country journal once wrote a column about
a typical Vermont dilemma. Which was better for starting the
fire in your wood stove, he pondered, the *New York Times* or the
Wall Street Journal?

New Hampshire is inhabited by real people who drive pickup trucks with gun racks and NRA bumper stickers; Vermont is a theme park full of Bostonians, New Yorkers, and Nebraskans dressed up in Vermont suits. When writers, intellectuals, violinists, and CEOs live north of Boston, they live in Vermont. If the oboe from the Indianapolis Symphony keeps a summer place back east, will it be a cottage on Lake Sunapee? If the chair of the mathematics department at Texas A & M drives five mornings into the sun from College Station for the month of August, does he aim for Penacook? In August Vermont drones with the sound of string quartets while motorcycle gangs converge on Laconia. (The rest of the year in New Hampshire it's the same noise, now performed by chainsaws and snowmachines.) Music festivals in Green Mountain towns, common as church suppers in New Hampshire, attract professors from the University of America, wearing checked shirts out of the L. L. Bean catalogue. Saturday mornings, while a native takes his trash to the dump, the collegial hayseed ties his Volvo to the old hitching post and swaps stories with the salty character who runs the general store this summer, who last year managed Kuala Lumpur for IBM.

In the 1995 census it was discovered that seventeen indigenous Vermonters remained in the state; twelve spent their winters in Florida with their running-to-the-dump money. The rest had migrated to New Hampshire, from Malltown to Milltown.

Meantime, in the world at large, a conspiracy denies New Hampshire's existence and implies that Vermont borders Maine. Vermont has become the generic name for any place north of Boston, unless it's got lobsters. At poetry readings I find myself invariably introduced as resident of an old family farm in Vermont. Five hundred people have written me letters, correctly addressed, in which they asked me how the weather was up there in Vermont. Twelve visitors have written us notes, after a week or a weekend, saying how much they enjoyed visiting us in Vermont.

In Vermont deer are required to have shots. In Vermont people keep flocks of spayed sheep to decorate their lawns. In Vermont when inchling trout are released into streams, a state law requires that they be preboned and stuffed with wild rice delicately flavored with garlic and thyme. Vermont has decorator barns; Calvin Klein will sign your woodshed for $250,000. In Vermont you can buy boots precaked with odorless manure. Taylor Rental outside Burlington hires Yankees out for parties, each guaranteed to know three hundred amusing rural anecdotes, all of them ending, "You can't get there from here." They chew nylon straw, they repeat "Ayuh" over and over again, and they cackle hideously until you pay them off. In 1998 TransUniversal Corporation acquired Vermont, reorganized it as Yankeeworld, and moved it to Arizona on flatbed tractors.

In New Hampshire the state supper is beans and franks, and every recipe begins with salt pork, Campbell's cream of mushroom, and Miracle Whip. In New Hampshire breakfast and supper are both at five o'clock. In New Hampshire a brunch is something not to walk into when you are hunting coon. In New Hampshire convenience stores sell Fluff, Wonder Bread, Moxie, and shoes with blue canvas tops. In Vermont they have the forty-hour work week; in New Hampshire the forty-hour work weekend is standard. In New Hampshire people work a hundred hours a week cutting wood, setting up the yard sale, and misdirecting flatlanders; the rest of the time they make Vermont maple syrup and Vermont cheese.

Vermonters who commute from Brookline in BMWs call New Hampshire folk rednecks. (*Redneck*, n., commonly used by liberals and college graduates to describe people who can drive a nail.) Patten Corporation completed paving Vermont in 1947.

It is true that parts of New Hampshire have already defected to other states: Salem is a suburb of Boston; Nashua is Silicon Valley with frost heaves; Winnipesaukee has been Coney Island for as long as Coney Island; Waterville Valley is a component of Aspen. It is true that we used to have a governor who wanted to nuke Massachusetts. It is true that New Hampshire is known nationally only for its early primary and its Live Free or Die license plate. Once every four years a New Hampshire citizen has a fifty-fifty chance to be interviewed on national television, and we are the only state so far to fulfill Andy Warhol's prophecy about everybody being famous for fifteen minutes. Once every four years the *New York Times*, *Time*, *Newsweek*, and *USA Today* send reporters to the Ramada Inn in Concord to file stories about desolation, political rigidity, fecklessness, and stale hors d'oeuvres.

New Hampshire's license plate motto comes from a revolutionary war hero, General John Stark, who may have been thinking more of Massachusetts than of George III. New Hampshire's obnoxious and independent bloody-mindedness derives from the seventeenth century, when the Bay Colony, sometimes abetted by London, tried to eat it alive. It derives also from the eighteenth, nineteenth, and twentieth centuries, as Massachusetts continues to cast cannibal glances north. Like the rural South, New Hampshire lives in a present that is the product of its history, and American history still lives in New Hampshire genes; mind you, we still vote for Frank Pierce.

Franklin Pierce, if you never noticed, was the fourteenth president of the United States, the only president from New Hampshire, and incidentally the only one not to be renominated by his own party after his term in office. If Rodney Dangerfield were authentic — and did not vacation in Las Vegas, Vermont — he would be Franklin Pierce. Vermont's only president, on the other hand, was Calvin Coolidge,* elected to the highest office because, as governor of Massachusetts, he suppressed strikes.

In Vermont the state flower is the sushi bar, and the state bird is the electric hot tub. In New Hampshire the state lunch is a submarine sandwich with a tub of coleslaw. Both are manufactured in the great coleslaw factories of Secaucus off the NJTP. Twenty-three years after his death, Robert Frost remains the poet laureate of Vermont;† like the rest of Yankeeland decoration, this poet laureate no longer functions, but he sure is cute. In Vermont, in 1999, the license plate slogan was Eat Three

---

* *New England Monthly* received five hundred and seven letters, all postmarked Vermont, indignantly reminding me that Chester A. Arthur was born in Fairfield, Vermont, on October 5, 1830. Actually it was 1831. Like many Vermonters, he became a New York machine politician.

† No longer true. In 1989, Galway Kinnell was named Vermont State Poet. We understand that Professor Kinnell lives on Bleecker Street in Greenwich Village.

Nutritious Meals a Day. In legislative committee this slogan edged out Experience Mozart.

Vermont plays double-A baseball in IBM's Burlington, as New Hampshire features the Nashua Pirates just off El Camino Real. But genuine New Hampshire folks play in the major leagues. Rich Gale won two games last year in Japan's World Series; he grew up in Littleton, with an effective summer season of thirty-eight days, counting Sundays. Still in the majors are Mike Flanagan, pitching for the Orioles, who like KC's Steve Balboni comes from Manchester; Joe Lefebvre of the Phillies, from Concord; and the great Carlton Fisk, most New Hampshire character of all, who grew up in the small Connecticut River town of Charlestown. It is rumored that one Vermonter clings to the roster of the California Angels.*

Not far north of Carlton Fisk's Charlestown, west and across the river, is Woodstock, Vermont, which just now lacks a representative in the major leagues. Woodstock is why I hate Vermont — and what I fear for New Hampshire. This is the Woodstock that Rockefeller money embalmed in the shroud of a small New England town: instant "Ye" at every parking lot; cute boutiques elbowing each other down main street; a dear old country inn fabricated in 1969. Nostalgia without history is a decorative fraud, and condosaurus, having consumed Vermont, munches at New Hampshire's borders.

---

* Most of this information is no longer true; it might as well be.

In 1986, as everyone remembers, the Boston Red Sox beat the New York Mets in the World Series, four games out of six. As the playoffs approached, the New York Times *sports section telephoned with a commission. I had listened to the radio all summer.*

THE RADIO
RED SOX

IN NORTHERN New England's September, as we drive past swamp maples turning red, we keep our radios tuned to the calm urgencies of Ken Coleman broadcasting from Fenway Park. This year the month was splendid not only for leaves.

The Red Sox belong to New England, not to the city of Boston. Of course, the region is diverse: Nothing but the name unites Danbury, CT with Danbury, NH where I live. We hear that there are areas in tropical Connecticut — where leaves do not turn until Thanksgiving — in which Yankees fans hold out like Japanese soldiers in island caves. There are even followers of some National League club from New York. But in our northern boondocks, the Red Sox contribute to regional identity, and it is by radio mostly that we follow our team. Deep in the country you don't get cable; the Red Sox TV channel in Boston is UHF.

In the old days, tangible baseball belonged to the villages, and the married men played the single men on the Fourth of July; the major league game happened in newspapers and in imagination. Among other consequences, this abstraction meant that you weren't required to root for Boston. You weren't stuck by radio and television with an omnipresent media team; you could pick for cherishing any team you wanted. Most folks followed a club nearby, but my uncle Dick, as a boy in Tilton, New Hampshire, before radio, followed the Cincinnati Reds — an imprinting similar to a baby duck's upon its mother. The great Cuban pitcher Adolfo Luque ("the Pride of Havana") inspired him (twenty years in the majors, twenty-seven and eight in 1923), and although he still allows grudging admiration for Jim Rice and Roger Clemens, his heart still throbs for a stadium near the Ohio River that he has never visited.

My New Hampshire grandfather, less aberrational, loved the Boston Red Sox for decades before he saw Fenway Park. Born in 1875, he took the train one Saturday in the 1890s to attend a professional game in Boston, National League, and recited that game in precious detail while he loaded hay onto a hayrack fifty years later. I heard about Hugh Duffy. In the meantime, he had switched his affection to the American League Red Sox, and every day at noon cherished yesterday's game in the *Boston Post* that came by mail. My grandfather imagined his own Ted Williams with glorious specificity, based on recollections of batting and fielding when he played the game himself. In those years we seldom heard games on radio. They played baseball in the afternoon while we were haying; if rain kept us from haying, it kept them from playing; on Sundays listening to the radio broke the Sabbath.

One day late in the 1940s my Connecticut father, on vacation with his in-laws, drove my grandfather and me down to Boston for a Wednesday afternoon game. My grandfather was so excited that round red spots like a clown's make-up fixed themselves on his high cheekbones. He saw the famous left fielder, old number 9. He watched his shortstop, his first baseman, his tall, left-handed pitcher — and he saw enormous Fenway Park with its vast throng of maybe ten thousand. The expedition was a success and in no way did it deepen my grandfather's affection for baseball and the Red Sox. Baseball was *there* always, an eternal game eternally stretched for the seventh inning, and when we paused for breath in the hayfield, my grandfather's clear storytelling voice would bring Smokey Joe Wood together with Johnny Pesky, Cy Young and Tris Speaker together with Mel Parnell, eternal teammates on the shadowy all-star team of a farmer's daydream. And this daydream was not merely private; it was social. Everybody talked baseball, even at town meeting in March. At the Grange or the post office in April, or on Old Home Day in August, my grandfather talked baseball with his old friends. Country people with horses and buggies did not see a great deal of one another, and when they met, the Red Sox formed a port of reentry for old conversations.

Things have not altogether changed. Now when we park the car and leave the motor running to pick up a cup of coffee at the Kearsarge Mini-Mart, old conversation continues in new mouths: "Did you hear that tenth inning last night?"

We get to Fenway more than once in forty years, but if we drive two to six hours to get there, it's hard to make the journey often. We rely on Ken Coleman and Joe Castiglione, the radio game with its background of noises, vendors and heckling, the rise and swoop of public hope and despair. Regular listeners learn to decode the announcer's pitch pattern, so that when bat-crack meets crowd-roar, Ken Coleman's first words, "Buckner hits a long . . . ," tell me *single, fly out,* or *possible home run* long before his words announce it.

Coleman is sixty-one and has broadcast thirty-one seasons of major league baseball with a soft attentiveness and the gentlest irony in the eastern United States. He's not given to false enthusiasm, artificial excitement, or gross charm. He's literate, friendly, and dependable; you trust the man, and that's how we want it. He brings the game in its folds and creases every day to millions of people driving pickups, milking cattle, and baiting traps, also to people drinking beer in barrooms, lazing on the beach, clipping coupons, and grooming polo ponies. Sixty-six New England stations carry the games, and everybody listens. The Red Sox with their beautiful archaic park are a radio team. Doubtless it is regional prejudice that makes the Mets, viewed from the north, seem as slick as network television.

Radio fans want to visit Fenway also; it's a validation. This year, we finally got there on September second and watched the Sox play Texas. Our seats were on the left-field foul line close to the wall. I could interfere with a ball without leaving my seat. O Fenway Park! (With some box seats in my uncle Dick's Cincinnati, you need binoculars to see home plate.) A few feet below us, we saw Gary Ward of Texas grab a single barehanded and snap it into second; we gazed as Jim Rice positioned himself to play a double off the wall like Bill Russell rebounding. We eavesdropped on the rage of their concentration. We watched their eyes.

We won. We came from behind and won it, eight to six. Al Nipper had some troubles, which allowed us a brief tour of the Boston bullpen, first Sammy Stewart and then Calvin Schiraldi, who relieved our anxieties with two strikeouts. But the high point of the evening was a walk. The Fenway crowd is knowledgeable, and the excitement — how do you explain this to a lover of football? — rose like a balloon as Wade Boggs, facing a left hander who gave him trouble, fouled off strike after strike in the seventh inning until he worked a walk that set up Marty Barrett's two-run single. Fourteen pitches.

When the game was over, we drove back to New Hampshire, our headlights reflecting the fires of autumn as we hit the north country. Sleepy the next day at the filling station, we heard a neighbor ask, "Did you see Boggs get that walk?"

"New Hampshire is known nationally only for its early primary." Therefore, Harper's *asked me to report on the scene during the campaign of 1987 leading to the 1988 primary and election. "Eagle Pond Letter," they called it.*

LIVING ROOM
POLITICS

ON ROUTE 4 most houses raise an orange or a blue newspaper tube beside rural delivery's mailbox. These colors record party affiliation, like the royal blue in northern Greece after World War II; blue tubes take New Hampshire's ultra-right *Manchester Union Leader*, and orange tubes the liberal *Concord Monitor*. Now, in late summer of 1987, every newspaper, every day, mixes local news with national politics as candidates attend Rotary breakfasts, Old Home Day parades, and senior citizens' coffee hours. In photographs every day we watch Senator Bob Dole hoist an obligatory baby; we see Congressman Dick Gephardt smile as he shakes a hand.

Some years back, an ex-governor of Georgia started visiting New Hampshire three years or so before the primary he was aiming at. Now campaigning has become full-time, but it hots up in the summer before the critical February primary. By July of last year, 1988's candidates swarmed as thick as blackflies in May. Weekly papers, with columns by stringers resident in each hamlet, took notice, mixing the domestic with the national. In August Sam Bigelow, who writes about Andover for Franklin's *Journal-Transcript*, varied the usual item ("Welcome back to Don and Jackie Hazen, returning after a two-week trip down South") by announcing:

> The Merrimack County Republican Committee will hold its annual barbeque picnic next Saturday from 2:00 to 5:00 P.M. at the home of Paul and Sharon Nagy, Chase Hill Road. . . . Special guests, as of a couple weeks ago, included Congressman Jack Kemp, Dr. Pat Robertson, General Alexander Haig, and Neil Bush.

We could read the follow-up in the next Monday's *Concord Monitor:* General Haig and Congressman Kemp both disliked the White House peace plan for Nicaragua; Elizabeth Dole suggested that her husband is best qualified to become "the leader of the free world"; Kate Hislop, identified as "a little-known candidate," told us how we need to "cut the deficit, limit welfare, and deport illegal aliens"; Kemp answered questions about superconductors and the Persian Gulf; Haig punned, "Beware of Dole and Dole. It's only watered-down pineapple juice"; Pat Robertson, who canceled, sent two ex-Broncos (from Denver) to state his case; represented by his son, Vice President George Bush won the straw poll.

A week later the pretty town of Salisbury, on Route 4 a few miles south, celebrated its Old Home Day. This New Hampshire holiday, like everything else in New Hampshire, is a local option. Andover has none; Danbury and Wilmot hold theirs on sequent Sundays in August, each featuring Moulton's Band from Sanborton ("continuous since 1889") in concert. In 1987 Salisbury's Old Home Day took place on Saturday, August 15, with a parade, picnic, and presentation of awards. Vice President Bush dropped by — the same day he dropped by Londonderry, Hopkinton, Webster, and New London — to award a clock to the eighty-year-old citizen of the year and to honor a young woman who won a national scholarship.

The Old Home Committee started planning the day's events last March without considering a vice-presidential visit. Three weeks before the event the selectmen heard indirectly that Bush would like to take part. One selectman later allowed, "At first we were not inclined." Another explained, "We didn't want it to be their party and not our day." They went along when they decided that a vice president would add honor to the honorees.

In primary season we are spoiled rotten. Don Marquis's phone keeps ringing; he handles social studies for Nashua secondary schools, and he hears himself saying, "No, senator, no, I'm sorry. I told you, you can only speak to one assembly a year." We meet them all if we want to. The weekend after Salisbury's Old Home Day, Bruce Babbitt, the former governor of Arizona, spoke at Daniell Point in Franklin, confluence of the Merrimack and Pemigewasset rivers, and argued for a national sales tax to reduce the deficit. He met my uncle Dick Smart, registered Republican for fifty years, who had just switched parties and said how much he enjoyed the Democrats: He didn't have to wear a tie now; and in fifty years, he said, Republicans had never offered him wine.

The *Manchester Union* waited until December to choose Pete du Pont, the former governor of Delaware, from among the Republican candidates; until then, the *Union* seemed more interested in knocking the governor of Massachusetts, Michael Dukakis. Sixteen years ago the *Union* ran a successful campaign against another New England favorite son, Maine's Edmund Muskie. Now the front page thundered, "Dukakis has pulled off one of the fastest and most underhanded skimming operations on Massachusetts taxpayers in the history of political-money-grabbing." The issue was a pay raise.

Dukakis didn't seem to be around New Hampshire much last summer. Everybody else was. Gephardt would be at Dennis and Margie Fenton's one night soon; there was a number to call or you could just drop by. The *Union*, one August morning, reminded us that Kemp would debate Gephardt at a college in Manchester the day after next. In the column headed "Campaign '88," we also read that a 1984 campaign coordinator for Mondale had signed on with Senator Joseph Biden; Paul Laxalt of Nevada was meeting with advisers at Bretton Woods (two

days later he withdrew, and a month later, Biden); the previous
night Kemp attacked Dole again; Senator Albert Gore was to
meet with teachers in Concord for a 12:30 lunch on Thursday,
visit Daniell Point in Franklin for coffee at 4:00, and return to
Concord sipping more coffee at 6:30; and Senator Paul Simon
would hit the Country Way nursing home in Keene that day, at
6:00 meet the Democrats of Peterborough, at 7:30 more coffee
in Goffstown.

In the common mercantile metaphor, politics in most of the
country is wholesale; in New Hampshire it is retail. Wholesale
is television advertising. Retail is continual coffee in living
rooms. It's fortunate for the candidates that nobody in this state
stays awake after 9:00 P.M.

Which brings up, of course, the absurdity of this eccentric state's
taking so much importance on itself. Roy Blount, Jr., tells about
a Yankee who criticized the South for flying the Confederate
flag. The Yankee bragged that the North didn't need a flag, and
Blount answered that the North wasn't a *place*. New Hampshire
is a place — as Milledgeville is and Birmingham isn't — and
among other things it is the place of the first primary. Everybody
has stories to tell. Merle Drown's father, known all over New
Hampshire as the Cheese Man because he sold cheddar at all the
fairs, managed to slip a hunk to JFK in 1960; the inevitable letter
thanked him for "the welcome change from campaign fare."
Merle and his wife Pat both teach high school; dark-horse
candidates search out coffee hours with high school teachers.
Four years ago (eight? twelve?) they talked with Fred and
LaDonna Harris, with Annie and John Glenn. When Pat finished
talking with Annie, two aides came up to her: "What did you
talk about? What's your name?" Shortly thereafter Pat received
a letter addressing the issues mentioned. We *all* get letters; first
class mail outnumbers catalogues. Not since William Faulkner
wrote me four letters with four different signatures, all postmarked New York while he lived in Virginia, have I received so
many communications from important people.

Famous politicos cozy up to us, which infuriates flatlanders
from New York and Massachusetts — which makes it worth-

while. Mike Barnicle, who apes Jimmy Breslin for the *Boston Globe*, can be counted on: "New Hampshire is to the country what Barry Manilow is to good music." On the other hand, the *New York Times* tries writing prose. A few years back, Francis X. Clines visited Danbury, on "the curving emptiness of Route 4." He interviewed five people and reported their cynicism about politics and politicians; two said they wouldn't even vote. Back on Forty-second Street, of course, everybody rushes to the polls.

Governor John Sununu* of New Hampshire calls politics New Hampshire's second-favorite indoor sport. And one of our oldest. Dennis Fenton — at whose house Gephardt talked late last summer — is an Andover selectman, my second cousin, and a good Democrat. His political flavor goes back to our great-grandfather John Wells, the Copperhead who hated Lincoln although he fought for the North. Gephardt retailed politics in the Fenton living room because a Danbury blacksmith believed in states' rights one hundred and thirty years ago. When my grandfather and his siblings (Dennis's grandmother was Wesley's sister Grace) grew up, Democratic politics crowded the table with quarrels at noontime dinner and at supper. As I hear stories about nineteenth-century New Hampshire, everything seems political. When the South Danbury Debating and Oratorical Society met in 1897 — my grandparents courted there — the younger set sang songs, played the piano, recited pieces, and then debated, "Resolved: That the United States Should Cease Territorial Expansion."

Politics remains retail in New Hampshire because of our system of government and the history that established it. The state was founded on distrust of anybody you could not look in the eye. Settled by refugees from theocratic Massachusetts, New Hampshire has always struggled to keep its identity. The northwestern part, the upper Connecticut River Valley, was populated by emigrants from Connecticut and western Massachusetts who also resented control from afar — from central New Hampshire, for instance. Distrust of government, be it federal or state, decided

---

* The New Hampshire primary took Sununu from Concord, New Hampshire, to Washington, D.C., where he is chief of staff for the man he backed in 1988.

the way we govern ourselves. Our enormous legislature started late in the eighteenth century, to keep the upper valley from forming another state. The New Hampshire House of Representatives marshals four hundred members to govern a state whose population edged over a million just a couple of years ago. Everybody knows his representative; my grandfather, a Democrat among Republicans, was elected representative seventy-five years ago. Jimmy Phelps, down in Danbury, was elected selectman when he was nineteen, and ran for representative when he was twenty-seven; the people who voted him in had gone to school with him. We talk every Friday when I pick up my mail.

Like everybody else in the United States, we distrust politicians; unlike everybody else, we find it hard to avoid becoming politicians. There are so many offices. My cousin Forrest, another great-grandson of John and Martha Wells, is selectman in Danbury; his mother Edna spent twenty-one years being elected trustee over graveyards in Danbury. Once a year we elect these officers, the same day we convene at the town meeting to tax ourselves. If we don't like the way our roads are plowed, we vote out the town road agent whom we voted in the previous March.

Sometimes we hear that Boston television, beamed into southern New Hampshire with its dense population of Massachusetts emigrants, is changing New Hampshire politics. But ask Walter Mondale. Four years ago he skipped coffee hours in favor of ads on television while Gary Hart answered questions in living rooms, with predictable results. For some candidates the living rooms are the hard part. It was in a Claremont living room that Senator Biden, irritated at a question from a high school teacher, boasted about his IQ and misrepresented his academic record. On the whole, I suspect that these face-to-face encounters are good for the candidates. In New Hampshire's primary season, candidates look in people's faces, not into cameras, when they answer questions; the little red light does not snap off until the question is answered.

I arrived at the Fentons' house "to meet Dick Gephardt" just before seven-thirty. Cars were already dense; New Hampshire runs on its own time, the only place in the country where it is polite to be fifteen minutes early for dinner. The candidate was already there, wearing the uniform: blue suit and red tie. One hundred and twenty people ate cookies and drank coffee, standing around in the living room, dining room, kitchen, hallway, and garage. Congressman Gephardt shook hands: smiling, serious, presidential. Maybe *too* presidential? He has been criticized for looking like the president of the senior class. He spoke for ten or fifteen minutes and then answered questions. The first came from an old man who had just shelled out four thousand dollars for a corneal implant that took four hospital hours. Later questions concerned the arms race, Nicaragua, and the Persian Gulf war. Gephardt didn't evade the questions; it would have been hard to.

As I drove home late that night, at a quarter past nine, I thought about the privilege of the evening — to be repeated as other candidates would stand in other Andover houses, one of them doubtless our next president, addressing issues such as disarmament, import policy, the Gulf, and military adventurism. I like this privilege and I consider it useful. Newspapers set agendas, television photographs everything, but in New Hampshire we get to watch the candidates' eyes as they answer our questions; the rest of the country watches us watching.

Commissions from Yankee *and* Country Journal, Harper's *and
the* New York Times *sports pages, allowed me to blurt brief bulletins. When the* New England Journal of Public Policy *asked
for an essay, I could use more space. I allowed myself to consider
the culture of the countryside and the politics that grows in this
sandy soil.*

RUSTICUS

OLD NEW HAMPSHIRE Highway Number 4, incorporated by
an act of the New Hampshire legislature in the autumn of 1800,
wound out of Portsmouth, a seaport that once rivaled Boston,
drove west through Concord, north past Penacook, through
Boscawen, Salisbury, and Andover on its way to Lebanon and
the Connecticut River. These town names string history like
beads. The Penacook tribe assembled each year on the banks of
the Merrimack at the site of the present town. I grew up thinking
Boscawen an unusual Indian name; it is Cornish, the surname of
an admiral victorious over the French in the eighteenth century.
In Andover, land was granted to veterans of the Louisburg Expedition against the French, but the first house did not go up
until 1761, a year after the English conquest of Canada put an
end to Indian raids. We need no reminding, now, that Lebanon
is an Old Testament name.

Not that these New Hampshire towns lack a history of violence. At Penacook is the island in the Merrimack River where
Hannah Dustin killed ten Indians in 1697. Forty years old, she

was kidnapped from the village of Haverhill, in the Massachusetts Bay Colony, where she had given birth a week earlier. Her husband with their seven older children was working in the fields, Dustin nursing her infant under the care of a neighbor named Mary Jeff, when Abenakis attacked, burned her house, and brained her baby against a tree. The Indians took the two women into the forest, where they divided their prisoners into small groups, Dustin and Jeff companioned with a boy captured at Worcester. As the three captives began their journey north toward Canada, their guards were two braves, three squaws, and seven Abenaki children. While the Abenakis slept on the Merrimack island the three Bay Colonists stole their tomahawks and murdered all but one squaw and one boy who escaped. The three ex-prisoners prudently hacked up the corpses of their captors, and when they returned to Haverhill received a bounty of fifty pounds for each scalp.

Cotton Mather tells the story, which he heard from Dustin herself, who survived into her eightieth year. We meet her again in Francis Parkman, who spells the name Dustan, but I first heard the adventure from my grandmother, told with some difference in detail as a family story about a heroic ancestor. Around the time my grandmother died in 1975, the Liquor Commission of the state of New Hampshire contrived a Hannah Dustin commemorative bottle filled with bourbon: You twist her head off (as the Abenakis should have done) and pour yourself Kentucky's whiskey.

New Hampshire's state economy, without sales tax or income tax, is based on wickedness and ill health. The first state lottery was New Hampshire's in 1963; flatlanders buy truckloads of cheap cigarettes; a state monopoly keeps liquor cheap. Huge stores beside the interstates sell cases to visitors from Massachusetts, while highway signs primly warn about the dangers of drinking and driving. Novelty items, like the effigy of the female Indian killer, help New Hampshire's citizens avoid taxes. I begin my generalizations about the culture or ethos of northern New England by relating these two pieces of New Hampshire lore, with nothing in common except a woman's name and fiscal prudence. Perhaps if we add the woman of 1697 to her figurine

of 1975 and divide by two, the product is present New Hampshire.

My grandmother was born in this house in 1878, thirteen
years after her father moved here. The white farmhouse sits on
a busy two-lane country highway, although the original Cape
was presumably set back from the Grafton Turnpike (incorporated in 1804, not finished until 1811), which headed north after
Highway Number 4 turned toward the sunset at West Andover.
The saltbox went up in 1803, I assume on a wagon track where
men led oxen. It would not go so far back as Hannah Dustin, for
reasons that her adventure makes clear. Most settlement this far
inland took place after the Revolution. Troops mustered out and
migrated north from Massachusetts — doubtless including de
scendants of the Haverhill Dustins — or west and north from the
New Hampshire seacoast, for independence and a piece of land.
This house stands between Danbury and Andover in the town
of Wilmot, incorporated in 1817 out of scraps and patches, including Kearsarge Gore. It remains quiet despite the traffic; we
see only one other house from our house. We love our country
solitude, interrupted by church, shopping, and occasional callers
who stop by the dooryard; we love Mount Kearsarge, noble to
the south of us; Eagle Pond, placid to the west; Ragged Mountain rising east behind our woodshed . . . But we love best the
culture we live in, despite its bourbon figurines.

When I was asked to write about New England mind or spirit,
at first I thought, Fine. That's what I always write about. A
reservation followed quickly: What do I know about the mind
of Greenwich, Connecticut? or Fall River, Massachusetts? or
Nashua, New Hampshire, for that matter? How can I generalize
about New England if I cannot even generalize about New
Hampshire? The novelist George Higgins, who used to review
magazines in the *Globe* on Saturdays, once quoted Ada Louise
Huxtable on New England: "It's a very Calvinistic life," she said.
"It has beautiful symmetry and restrictions, and great intellectual elegance." Higgins was puzzled: Perhaps Huxtable had
overlooked Brockton and Lawrence? When Huxtable continued
by saying, "But you could say it's a little constipated," Higgins's

puzzlement disappeared. "It's Cambridge," he deduced with relief.

Surely he was correct. The New Hampshire in which I live is as alien to Cambridge as it is to Brockton, and it is about *this* province that I allow myself to speak. If what I observe in Wilmot, Danbury, and Andover applies elsewhere, it will apply mostly to other parts of northern New England — not to Nashua nor to the low-tax Boston suburb called Salem, New Hampshire — and spreading west from Vermont into the poorer rural regions of northern New York and Pennsylvania, into the country towns of eastern Ohio, settled with New Englanders about the time these New Hampshire towns were settled, with handsome village squares and Federal buildings.

Not to mention the rural South.

During the year, I take brief trips away from this house as I read my poems at colleges. Every year I go to the West Coast once or twice; I visit Texas once a year, not only Austin and Dallas but Lubbock and Waco; I visit the exotic landscapes of Idaho, Colorado, Montana, Oklahoma, and Utah; I return continually to the various institutions of Ohio — and nowhere in the United States am I reminded so much of rural New Hampshire as when I read my poems at small colleges in Georgia, Alabama, and South Carolina. In a circle surrounding Atlanta — which could almost be Toledo — small colleges inhabit middle-sized Georgia towns: Columbus, Augusta. When I stay at the Carrollton Holiday Inn, I might as well sleep in Rhode Island or Montana. But when I walk or drive outside Rome, Georgia, or when I sit on the verandah in Cross Hill, South Carolina, although the architecture differs, although the accent is incorrect, I feel homely emanations rising from the red dirt. Resemblance begins with the sculpture, alive in the center of southern towns as it lives in Wilmot Flat, of the Civil War soldier and the soldier of the War Between the States — slim fellow eternally bronze, standing alert with musket and identical standard handsome features, with the minor discrepancy of uniform, of victory and defeat.

He stands more often in the South than he does in New Hampshire. He poses in Wilmot Flat, not in Andover or Dan-

bury. Rich Andover raised a war monument only in 1923, five years after what the granite slab calls THE WORLD WAR, but the list of one hundred and forty-three Civil War soldiers takes pride of place on the monument's front. Poor Danbury — which my great-grandfather left for the New Hampshire Volunteers, Company F, 15th Regiment — fixes a small bronze plaque on the Town Hall. Among the fifty-one names, from Samuel S. Adams to Addison L. Woodman, I recognize families that survive in Danbury one hundred and twenty years later: Braley, Brown, Butler, Danforth, Farnham, Ford, Minard, Morrill, Morrison, Sanborn. I recognize the name of a cousin killed by cannonball at Vicksburg. My ancestor John Wells brought back to the cousin's family the contents of his pockets, and one object has come down to this house. I have already mentioned his ring of bone.

Only in small towns of the rural South and in northern towns of New England does this war survive: blockade, starvation, burning, attrition, sepsis, amputation, and charges into cannon fire. If you search the suburbs from Connecticut through New York and New Jersey, past Pennsylvania, skirting Gettysburg into Ohio, Michigan, and Indiana, if you search through the Plains states to the West Coast from Orange County to Bellevue, Washington, you will not find this war. In the present United States, this war recedes into olden times, like Homer, the Roaring Twenties, the Crusades, Gilgamesh, and Will Rogers. It is preserved like a bottled fetus in the library and in the notebooks of genealogical eccentrics. But outside Atlanta and Birmingham, and north of Boston, the blue and the gray still march, bugle call and amputated limb, in the fierce cannonade of old memory. The past continues into the present because the plaque's family names remain on the land. Only in the rural South and rural New England do you find Americans who live where their great-grandfathers lived, or who know the maiden names of their great-grandmothers.

Rural New Hampshire separates itself not only from Cambridge and Brockton. Let me call rural people a separate class, Class Rusticus. In order to talk of its uniqueness, I must speculate about the cultures against which it distinguishes itself. When we talk about American classes by making revision of European class structures, I suspect we miss the point. Americans divide themselves not so much into economic classes as into ethnic, regional, and cultural groups, except that most of us belong to a single class within which there is considerable economic hierarchy. Massclass is singular because it shares goals and values, and because it does not care where it lives except in connection with these desires. (The names of desired objects alter according to the hierarchy, and your mobile home is my year in France.) When I assert Massclass, I do not deny that poverty and suffering assault its unluckier members. Depression or recession, unemployment, bankruptcy and foreclosure, failure and social welfare, are cyclical components of our economy. I speak of the commonness not of success and prosperity but of standards of success and prosperity. Neither do I deny the existence of a separate underclass, perpetually burdened by poverty, rendered almost unemployable by habitual loss, generation after generation nurtured and enfeebled by welfare. (I only deny, by definition, that these sufferers may be called working class.) At the other extreme, maybe there are a few families, with money around for several generations, who make an American upper class. Maybe. I remain skeptical of an inherited upper class in the United States, skeptical that its narcissism is secure. These people hold to superiority over rich Massclass managers only by the skin of their capped teeth, the way the lower middle class in older Europe paddled furiously to distinguish itself from workers. Black is a class, most of the time, a culture and a set of values distinct from Massclass from which some blacks emigrate into Massclass. I suppose that Hispanic is another. Emigrant is a one-generation class, culturally divided according to place of origin, the second and third generation joining Massclass America.

This digression means to claim: Rusticus is another class or culture; I live among this class as a Massclass emigrant. My mother and my grandmother were born in this house but my mother moved to Hamden, Connecticut — a suburb of New Haven — when she married, and I grew up among blocks of similar houses, a neighborhood where everyone shared four convictions: 1. I will do better than my father and mother. 2. My children will do better than I do. 3. "Better" includes education, and education exists to provide the things of this world. 4. The things of this world are good.

Within my Connecticut town the neighborhoods were distinct, and they were distinct according to hierarchies of money — the market value of houses, their size and proximity to each other, the number of stalls in their garages. In Hamden we lived on the western side of Whitney Avenue in a prosperous section called Spring Glen, a little more prosperous than Whitneyville, richer than Centerville and State Street. Because we were on the western side of Whitney, my father always said we lived on the "two-bit side"; east of Whitney was the "fifty-cent side." If I enjoy myself in ironies about Massclass, it is not with the notion that I thereby detach myself. I am a card-carrying member, Amexco, and one does not alter the habits and values of a lifetime by changing one's place of residence. I retain the markings: distaste for physical labor, fear and loathing of false teeth, desire for my children's education and comfort. Because my parentage was mixed, because I spent my childhood summers in this house, I kept at least a vision of something different.

The class or culture of Rusticus is alien to Massclass. Let us start with a stereotype of New Hampshire's citizenry as cherished by citizens of Boston: Rusticus women are fat; Rusticus men wear crew cuts; there isn't a full set of God-given teeth from Vermont's border on Lake Champlain eastward to Maine's Atlantic coast. Mr. and Mrs. R. inhabit a thirty-year-old trailer without calling it a mobile home, surrounded by two junked Buicks and a pickup that's all froze up next to the old freezer past the washing machine; they're somewhere between thirty-two years old and fifty-seven, but it's hard to tell; each weighs two hundred and twelve pounds, but he spreads his weight over his whole five foot eight and a half inches while she tends to be more concentrated at five foot one; the working truck wears a gun rack and an NRA bumper sticker; there's a sign for night crawlers and another for a yard sale; when the mill's going they gum Twinkies and TV dinners, but when they're laid off they settle for squirrel meat and potato chips; they have never applied for food stamps be-

cause they don't know they are poor and because people on welfare are liars and cheats. They vote Republican.

When Massclass visitors honor Rusticus with the epithet "redneck," they acknowledge an analogy to the rural South, and
acknowledge as well the antipathy that one class or culture feels
for another. "Redneck" is racist slang, like "hillbilly"; it demon-
strates urban and suburban superiority while it conceals fear of
the alien. But of course Massachusetts liberals, when they speak
of the rednecks of New Hampshire, do not believe that they
demonstrate fear of overweight people without teeth. They feel
that they denounce right-wing politics, narrow and bigoted opinions associated with Alabama sheriffs named Virgil who shoot
SNCC workers. These flatlanders may assemble some evidence
to support their bigoted generalizations. There *was* a New Hampshire governor who praised the living conditions of Soweto; there
is a newspaper that is not only the worst moment of journalism
in the United States, but the most grossly conservative. But things
are never so simple as our righteousness makes them out to be.
Even to characterize New Hampshire's politics as right wing is
unhistorical, as if we called Hannah Dustin a racist for her position on the question of Native American rights.

Reading early American history, one becomes aware that the
Revolution started not with the shot heard round the world but
with the seventeenth-century landings at Virginia and Plymouth. It started with the extraordinary, habitual independence
of these colonies from their sovereign across the sea. Our ancestors were ungovernable from abroad; they were also largely
ungovernable at home. Within each colony, every unit separated
itself as much as possible from every other unit — town from
state, village from town, family or neighbor-group from village,
and legislature from governor. On occasion we had to cooperate:
to fence the common, to build a jail. *Some* law was necessary,
but in spirit most colonists, Puritan or not, remained grossly an-
tinomian. We were, after all, self-selected separators, alike only
in that we all decided to leave the past behind and start over.

New Hampshire's history for three hundred years — I need
to say it again — has been dominated by the necessity to separate
itself from its rich neighbor. If New Hampshire had not made

itself a porcupine, Massachusetts would have swallowed it alive. The generally separatist tendencies of Americans were exacerbated for New Hampshire by the power of Boston. When colonies became states, when the Union needed preserving, still Franklin Pierce's Democrats voted in the House against using federal funds for construction of highways and canals in states and territories. Ideas of states' rights, and states' consequent responsibilities, pertained not only to slavery and the South.

Although my great-grandfather was a Copperhead — like the New England fellow who named his son Robert Lee Frost after moving west to California along with others who bet on the wrong side — John Wells fought for the Union out of local feeling. He never spoke of the war, hated Lincoln all his life, and bequeathed to his posterity genetic adherence to the Democratic party, which leaves my family, out of loyalty and DNA, eccentric in New Hampshire. When the Democrats nominated Al Smith, John Wells's offspring decided that the pope would not take over the West Wing; Roosevelt's New Deal seemed only sensible to the clan descending from John Wells.

Not so for my neighbors in general, skeptical not only of national government but of bigwigs in the state capital and, if truth be known, of the selectmen they themselves elect on town meeting day. If this politics is right wing, what do we call the National Association of Manufacturers, General Motors, ABC Television, conglomerates and cartels, *US News*, or Ronald Reagan? Of course New Hampshire Republicans are conservative in their anticollectivism, but Reagan Republicans are collectivists of capitalism, and agribusiness is corporate collective farming, and U.S. Steel is stockholder nationalization.

In New Hampshire the ideal remains to work for yourself. Units of one are preferred: one-family mill, one-family farm, one-woman peddler, and one-man logger. Veteran hippies move in, turning Libertarian in a climate that is almost anarchic. All political labels falsify when they try to name particular cases. I think of an old friend in Danbury, in his late eighties now, salty as the Atlantic, who fought for his country in the Great War. At some point in his sixties he found in his mailbox a pension check — and he was infuriated. He sent it back with an insulting note. What was *this* for? Did the government suppose that he fought for his country in order to be paid for it? He was a Republican for sixty years; Nixon changed that. Now he knows (and he feels foolish that he didn't always know): They are all scoundrels. Perhaps they are — and when we do not organize, we are helpless against them; one person, or a series of ones, battles without weapons against a corporation, as we discover when cotton mills or landfills become profitable.

In the conservatism of Rusticus there is considerably more Thomas Jefferson than Alexander Hamilton, yet New Hampshire's voters pile up majorities for Reagan's banks, deficits, and big business. Political labels deny manyness and complexity. If Lincoln's Republicans were radical on slave territory, they were conservative to maintain the Union; if the secessionists were conservative of slavery, they were radical to secede. Radical and traditional. Magnolias, honor, Tara, and pure women erected a political lie of nobility to cover evil, the usual lie that helps us to think well of ourselves, to call ourselves good when we are vicious. Nineteenth-century chattel slavery — slavery in 1860 — was morally as defensible as the Final Solution. The courage of evil is an imperial commonplace.

In the ethics of Rusticus, the noble lie that masks evil is Proud Independence. We cannot compare this vice to slavery, pogroms, or napalmed villages, but it is worth acknowledging that our freedom from taxation imposes suffering on the poor, on the insane, and on the otherwise handicapped; that New Hampshire, refusing to fund Medicaid, ruins families with ill children; that laissez faire with its abhorrence of zoning allows corporations to own dumps that murder ponds and probably people; that Proud Independence is an illusion of the many that serves the greedy few.

Not that notions of independence are without cultural benefit. For one thing, the culture of Rusticus encourages eccentricity, and eccentricity valued promotes the acceptance of diversity. Three quarters of the stories I hear — "Did you hear about the time old Meacham made skunk stew?" — celebrate divergent behavior; a few famous eccentrics, dead fifty years, get talked about every day in Danbury. Social results of this enthusiasm are varied and useful. In the countryside, and never in the suburb, old and young live next to each other, rich and poor, foolish and shrewd, educated and semiliterate. As in the country the sexes have traditionally separated their workloads less, as there has been less hierarchy among trades and occupations, so sparseness of population mixes neighbors at random, and the trailer or the shack squats two hundred yards down the road from the extended, huge late-eighteenth-century farmhouse spruced up with fresh paint on clapboard and shutters. At church and store, garage and rummage sale, the neighbors in their variety talk with each other. In the neighborhoods of Massclass, suburban ghettos quilt-patterned with hierarchy, old and young are as separated as rich and poor. Alienation breeds fear that wears the costume of contempt.

The social ethic of this varied Rusticus culture is niggardly in public and charitable in private; generosity is permitted as long as it appears voluntary, whimsical, responsive, and unplanned. Ideas of work live at the center of this ethic, and the finest Rusticus compliment is "She's not afraid of a day's work," pronounced *wuk*. Variety of competence is as valuable as diligence. Half of Rusticus men can build a house from cellar to shingles. Such versatility is historical. In the old days everybody was a farmer, including preacher and lawyer and doctor, and every farmer could turn a lathe or operate a forge. Further back, the farmer made shoes winter evenings while his wife made clothing. She began with the sheep's wool or flax fibers; she dried or carded, she spun, wove, cut, and sewed; she ended with dress, with trousers, with workshirt. Grandfather and grandmother Rusticus were part-time everything — wagon maker, candle maker — and their descendants remain jacks-and-jills-of-all-trades, unlike the specialist citizens of suburbs and cities.

On the old general farm — eight Holsteins, fifty sheep, two hundred chickens, five pigs; ice cut from the pond in winter to cool the milk of summer; cordwood cropped for heat and cooking, for canning and sugaring and probably for sale; vegetables raised for the summer table and for canning; fieldcorn grown for the cattle's ensilage — man and woman worked equally hard. The women who worked just as hard as the men neither voted nor as a rule owned property. Nonetheless, it is not merely ironic to speak of egalitarianism in the workload of the sexes, because work makes pride and equality of labor confers value. Of all the aggressions on the female inflicted by male industrial culture, surely the most destructive was enforced decorative leisure, useless ornamentation, despairing conspicuous inutility. In the growth of capitalism, the sexes in the middle and upper classes specialized: Men worked as women demonstrated by their leisure men's prosperity. This arrangement drifted down from aristocrats — where the man was equally burdened with uselessness — to the urban middle class in the late eighteenth century and became epidemic in the nineteenth century, along with female neurasthenia. Middle-class women were not allowed to do anything useful, and if their males died or failed or went crazy or alcoholic, there was no system of support — proving again the importance of males. As late as the 1930s, when my mother left the farm and accommodated herself to the Massclass life of Connecticut, wives did not take jobs. She had been a teacher, and only virgins taught school. Although my father's weekly wage was small, maybe thirty-five dollars, it was the Depression: As part of her acclimatization, my mother hired a girl, five dollars a week, to clean house, cook, and serve dessert for bridge on Wednesdays in a black dress with a tiny white apron over it.

Her mother, at the same age, made soap. Every night the whole family gathered in a circle around a high table with an oil lamp on it, as the women sewed socks, basted hems, knitted mittens, crocheted, and tatted. While the mother ruled her house-empire of power, the father remained all day outside in his domain of barns and sheds. Think of my mother growing up in this world and after the brief transition of college moving to Connecticut where the maid picked up the teacups after bridge on Wednesday afternoons. It is true that she ironed seven white shirts a week for her husband and seven more for her son. It is also true that on the New Hampshire farm, her mother sometimes hired help. When crews worked at harvest, my grandmother hired a woman who lived nearby to make pies all morning for ten cents an hour. Because this helper valued her self-esteem, she would go home in the early afternoon, eighty cents richer, change into fancy clothes, and return as a neighbor for whom my grandmother would construct a cup of tea.

This story reminds me of an anecdote Henry James tells. When he wrote *The American Scene*, returning from decades of English life to his brother William's summer place in Chocorua, he wrote lyrically of landscape — and with amused horror of New Hampshire's egalitarianism. New Hampshire lacked "the squire and the parson." Henry missed measure and order; he lamented "the so complete abolition of *forms*." He appears shocked, for our entertainment, as he tells about a rustic, to whom he ascribes cynicism, "who makes it a condition of *any* intercourse that he be received at the front door." This rustic asks the summer person who opens the door, "Are you the woman of the house?" in order to deliver a message from someone he calls the "washerlady."

This is a story about manners, and therefore about *form*, like my grandmother's pie maker who turns up at teatime. In James's anecdote, the characteristic teasing humor of Rusticus is accomplished by careful misuse of language. (New Hampshire humor is always verbal: One common form derives from literalness: "Why is Dean pulling that big chain?" "Ever see anybody trying to *push* one?" Another is self-mockery of proverbial cautiousness: "Say, is Cal Morey your brother-in-law?" "Well, he was this morning.") When I lived in Ann Arbor, I suffered from the manners of ironic deference. People deferred to me because I wrote books, an activity with prestige in the academy, where worth is measured by column inches of bibliography; they fell into irony because they could not abide their own deference. Living on Route 4, I suffer from no such burden. It seems not to occur to anyone that I might think myself better than they are because I write books. Why should it be better to write books than to build houses or grow blueberries? Better is not an issue. I am doing what I want to do and what I can do; so are other people, if they are sensible and fortunate.

Not that Class Rusticus is without its own systems of superiority. If it were not known that I worked hard, I would feel disapproval. The general ethic praises work, and hard-working pillars of the community find laziness contemptible. Naturally

there are lazy people about, working now and then in harvest or
cutting summer brush on a ski slope or shoveling snow in February — feckless, agreeable, sitting around in the summer twilight
with a six-pack. I mean to distinguish the self-appointed bum
from the unlucky, from the insulted and injured, from the con-
genitally unemployable *poor*. Of course it is commonplace for
Rusticus as Republican to deny the distinction.

Women of the rural culture remain indistinguishable as workers from the men. Bum-women lie about with their six-packs;
pillar-women work fourteen hours, and now, like their men,
labor at factory jobs before they come home to continue working. The forty-hour week is unknown; Rusticus works either
eighty hours a week or none. If I brag to a neighbor that I have
just frozen sixty pints of tomatoes, I hear a counterboast that puts
me in my place: four hundred and eighty pints, of everything.
A forty-hour week may pay the mortgage or the taxes; then we
are free to improvise, to do what we want to do, to raise pigs and
cut cordwood, fish through the ice, sharpen saws, tear down a
barn, hunt deer, build a house. In the nineteenth century, farm
boys took jobs at the hame shop in Andover because they had to
work only twelve hours a day, six to six, only six days a week,
and they paid you real money for it; it was a week on Hampton
Beach compared to the farm. When the boss turned soft, around
the turn of the century, and closed the shop at noon on Saturday,
old-timers were contemptuous: "That's not a week's wuk!"

Once this ethic of work was common in the United States,
when most people lived outside cities. Even Hamden was a town
of farmers providing milk and produce for the port of New
Haven. In the eighteenth century, Eli Whitney used water power
(at the outlet of today's Lake Whitney, alongside Whitney
Avenue) for his gun factory. When he built houses for his workers, Whitney's Village became Whitneyville, the section of Hamden where my father grew up. My great-grandfather Charlie
Hall labored building the New Haven Reservoir in 1861, off
Armory Street in Hamden near the old Whitney factory, and at
noon he walked off his job and trudged three miles into New
Haven, where he enlisted to fight for the Union. When he died
during another war, in 1916, his Hamden had altered from a

small town into a suburb of New Haven. It took another forty years and another war to complete its transformation. Hamden High School shot up in a farmer's field half a mile from our house in about 1940. After 1945 and victory came the Hamden Plaza farther down Dixwell, then the Hamden Mart, acres of shiny stores surrounding macadam parking lots that blacked over old farmland. In the 1960s and 1970s condominiums arose behind the stores, high on the hills overhead; traffic lights blossomed everywhere, bustle and confusion and change. By 1990 the shopping malls have turned dingy. Our history becomes thirty seconds of film collage, not slow like Eisenstein or a Marx Brothers movie, but accelerated like *Laugh In:* accelerated decay, decline, defeat. In Whitneyville where I watched the huge (as I thought) brick Brock-Hall building rise when I was in kindergarten, wreckers and bulldozers have leveled it and another condominium rises. Next door where I attended the opening of the Whitney Theater before the war, dozers wait to knock down the theater and the little row of shops beside it on Whitney Avenue in Whitneyville to make way for more condos. After condosaurus has ruled its moment, some disaster will wipe it out. Another creature will walk in its place while its cinderblock bones sink on top of Eli Whitney's gun workers' cottages and the bones of shaggy dairy horses.

Henry James in *The American Scene* spoke of New York as a "vision of waste" because of the destruction of good houses, "marked for removal, for extinction, in their prime." New York was vanguard and template. John Jay Chapman (1862–1933) was a New Yorker who admired the exuberance of his town but who had been modified by Massachusetts after a tour at Harvard. "New York is not a civilization," he wrote, "it is a railway station. . . . The present in New York is so powerful that the past is lost. There is no past. Not a bookshelf, nor a cornice, nor a sign, nor a face, nor a type of mind endures for a generation, and a New York boy who goes away to boarding school returns to a new world at each vacation." On the other hand, "In Massachusetts you may still stop the first man you meet in the street and find in his first remark the influence of Wyclif. . . . It is one-sided, sad, and inexpressive in many ways. But it has coherence."

If we consult George Higgins about "the influence of Wyclif," he may question our experience of Brockton. Nor would one find much coherence, now, even on Beacon Hill. New York is model for city and suburb from sea to shining sea. When Thomas Hardy wrote a preface to *Far from the Madding Crowd*, twenty-seven years after its first publication, he wailed a familiar complaint of alteration and loss. After lamenting the disappearance of rural customs, he went on:

> The change at the root of this has been the recent supplanting of the class of stationary cottagers, who carried on the local traditions and humours, by a population of more or less migratory labourers, which had led to a break of continuity in local history, more fatal than any other thing to the preservation of legend, folk-lore, close inter-social relations, and eccentric individualities. *For these the indispensable conditions of existence are attachment to the soil of one particular spot by generation after generation.*

My italics. The unhistorical may smile at the date of 1895; the present's creature thinks that, because people complained a hundred years ago as they complain today, the complaint must be constant and not the matter complained of. But a hundred years is a wink of historical time. Hardy's complaint was valid in 1895 and it is valid now.

What surprises me, I suppose, is the holding out, for despite Hardy's pessimism, and my own when I was young, there is resistance to the murder of the past. Rusticus is a series of eccentric individualities, complete with legends and folklore, and this culture will persist at least into the 2000s.

Italian hill towns, settled by Greek colonists long before Christ, spoke ancient Greek halfway through the twentieth century. In New Hampshire we still speak Greek. Over the decades of Hamden's destruction, the look of the land around Eagle Pond has altered but not greatly. When I alighted at the West Andover depot in 1939, my grandfather drove Riley and the buggy past a series of dying one-man farms. The farms and the men and the horses and the depot are dead, and stone walls that once marked pastures for a few cattle now keep pine trees from wandering into Route 4. But the houses mostly endure. In the culture of

Rusticus, tearing things down is as wicked as fecklessness. Nothing separates Massclass from Rusticus more than rural dedication to preservation and continuity. When the University of Michigan, inheriting a beautiful Federal house on State Street in Ann Arbor, sold it so that it was torn down for a fast-food franchise — I did not make this up! — there was only a resigned shaking of heads.

Returning here, I told myself that I returned to house, hill, and pond, the nonhuman environment, and that, after all, my work was such that I could do it anywhere. Of course, I discovered or rediscovered that the people were dearer than the hills. (I had not suspected so, I think because I had made a decision in my twenties not to live here. In the spirit of Aesop's fox, I disparaged the New Hampshire present.) When I came back in 1975, to live where I wished to live, I found myself among other people who live where they do because they wish to and for no other reason. Ann Arbor (Berkeley, Madison, Hamden, Atlanta, and Shaker Heights) is largely composed of people who live where they live because that's where the job is. They will leave when a better job comes along elsewhere, the migrating laborers of prosperous Massclass. There's a commonplace, repeated at parties in Ann Arbor, that is standard on every campus of the University of America: "One third of the people in this room were not in town last year; one third will not be here next year." The words go unspoken in Danbury.

Rusticus lives where he does because he wants to. Anybody with a skill and an appetite for work can make more money elsewhere. People who build houses can get twice as much an hour if they emigrate two hours south. Many leave to follow the money; then they return, shaking their heads, surprised that they will put up with less income for the sake of place, determined to do just that: not martyrs, just un-Americans of happy voluntary low income. People who remain here are self-selected partisans of place. Many were born here, after parents, great-grandparents, and great-great-grandparents. Many moved here because they liked the look and feel of it. Some came here because of a job and then refused to be transferred elsewhere. They are un-American because they prefer land, place, family, friends, and culture to the possibilities of money and advancement. Doubtless many Americans prefer something or other over money, but most of us feel guilty when we do anything except for money; we think that a man is not manly or decisive if he admits a motive outside money. But no one remains in rural New Hampshire for the money. Everybody living here hangs out a sign: *I don't care so much for money as I'm supposed to.* Therefore Massclass, in the shape of summer people, laughs at the native, and the native, secure in a secret superiority, laughs back. This is the cynicism of Henry James's rustic.

Indifference to money is not proof of virtue; ax murderers are notoriously indifferent to the wages of their profession. It depends on what you love instead of money, or on the mix of motives. Many people remain here not only out of love but out of dependence or perhaps inertia. Maybe it is happy to be place-bound or family-bound, but it limits one's chances to become a ballet dancer or an astronaut. In my family that has stayed here forever, I hear this limitation in many stories. Aunt X started normal school over to Plymouth, an hour away, but took sick and came home and never did go back: homesick. Uncle Z, with a job in a sawmill, worked only part-time because the mill was doing poorly; his weekly wage was minuscule. He found a job four hours west in Vermont, doing the same work at twice the money. Soon he was back at the old New Hampshire job, making do and looking for odd jobs to buy shoes for his children. He missed his brothers and his old mother.

Still, the love of place shows itself noble and honorable in a hundred ways. We returned to an 1803 house, including an unrevised 1803 chimney, which had gone with insufficient maintenance during my grandmother's eighties and nineties. I have mentioned that as we shingled, painted, replaced a chimney, and repaired, people constantly thanked us: "*Good* to see the old place coming back." It was extraordinary, this public delight in our restoration. Strangers parked their cars, as we worked in the garden, to praise us for keeping the old house alive.

The land (not the scenery) is dearer than I credited. Once at our church, our summer minister — pushing eighty, he lives in the farmhouse he was born in — asked us to come next week

prepared to speak about something in the Creation that we liked
to look at. The next Sunday he could hardly get his sermon in, as
his normally taciturn parishioners gabbled their passions: the
Jack Wells Brook where it dropped over the little rapids; the
noble stretch of double stone wall by Frazier's place; the patch
of wild daylilies at the base of New Canada Road; the way Kearsarge changes color in dawn light month by month all year,
green and blue and white and lavender; the gaunt and bony
ruin of an old mill foundation.

The main link that joins us together, and separates country
people from Massclass, that ties rural North to rural South, is
connection to the past. We love the house, not just for its lines or
its endurance, but because of people who were born and died
here; we love the mountain, not only because it's beautiful, but
because we know that the dead gazed at it every day of their lives
and left behind testimony of their love. House and mountain
connect us to the past. These connections may be strongest for
true Rusticus, but these feelings do not require blood ties; blood
ties only facilitate them. These connections are also strong for
emigrants from Massclass who join themselves to the rural
culture because they cherish its connectedness. They prevail not
only among the inhabitants of white farmhouses but among
shack people who approach the flatlander's stereotype. Not all
shack people, of course; not all green-shutter people either . . .
but connections in this culture *prevail*.

In the last decade or two, all the little towns have started historical societies (I belong to the Danbury, Wilmot, Andover,

and Northfield historical societies), which meet sometimes for invited speakers with special knowledge — railroads, Shakers, watermills — more often with a neighbor who brings photographs to show and stories to tell. Historical societies sponsor museums: In the Wilmot Town Hall, in the Flat, we keep a room with old photographs, Civil War memorabilia, old farm tools, clothing, flags, and typed-up reminiscences; in Andover the elegant Potter Place Depot, a glory of Victorian gingerbread, was donated to the Andover Historical Society as a museum. The depot itself is exhibit number one.

Historical societies may be fads, like the gentrification of old quarters in cities, but really they may represent deep mind-habits: They are storytelling turned into institutions. The section of Andover called Potter Place took its name from Richard Potter, celebrated magician and ventriloquist of the early nineteenth century, who spent his show-business fortune to build a mansion in Andover, which burned when my mother was a girl. He died before the railroad came, but when the new railroad built a depot near his house, the depot was named Potter Place. More than a hundred years after his death my grandfather told me trickster stories about Richard Potter as a "fellow used to live around here," who avenged himself on an enemy farmer by hiding in the bushes and casting his voice so that the brute heard a baby crying from his load of hay, emptied his hayrack, loaded it again, heard the baby cry again . . . My grandfather neglected to mention one piece of information about Richard Potter: either he did not know or it seemed unimportant that he was black.

In most of the United States you do not hear stories about a "fellow used to live around here" one hundred and fifty years ago. In most of the United States, you know that the lawn you water was desert or apple orchard or strawberry field until 1957 — and that is all you know. We Americans dislike the past. Or we simply adore it and lump it all together as a glossy product of generalized nostalgia, *olden times*, a decorative and disconnected alternative to the present. The ornamental past enforces the dominance of the temporary.

W. H. Auden remarked that the mediocre European is pos-

sessed by the past and the mediocre American by the present.
One must admit that many of the cleverest and most inventive
Americans — Benjamin Franklin, Thomas Jefferson — were possessed by the present. Ralph Waldo Emerson, with centuries of
accumulated knowledge and culture enlightening and burden-
ing him, spent a lifetime celebrating our independence of history,
authority, religion, and order; his intelligence served American
disconnections. But if many bright Americans are possessed by
the present, all dumb Americans are. An unexamined assump-
tion of Massclass is that such possession is a duty, and the result
is the torn-down Federal house.

In northern New England, in Wendell Berry's Kentucky, and
in other rural places, the culture suggests and supports connection to a continuous past that lives in the air, in relics, and in the
stories that old people tell. Everywhere are antiquarians, but
without the linkage of stone wall and Civil War soldier in bronze,
and without the same soldier in story, library antiquarianism is
documentary and disconnected. It is better than nothing, because
it gives evidence of our famine, of our need for the nutrition of
historical connection against the thin, bare, accelerated moment.
Perhaps the recovery of old quarters in Chicago, Washington,
and Boston is not merely faddish but testimony of true hunger.

Americans can almost be defined as people who lack history,
who emigrated here to escape a nightmare from which they
could not awake. Current protests about the unhistoricism of the
American young repeat and multiply complaints that started before the Revolution, complaints that the successful and blessed
Revolution only accelerated. But a narrower present turns into
a worse nightmare, and as always we divorce for the same reasons that marry us. In *The American Scene*, still in New Hampshire, Henry James spoke of the land "not bearing the burden of
too much history." But he continued:

The history was there in its degree, and one came upon it, on
sunny afternoons, in the form of the classic abandoned farm of
the rude forefather who had lost patience with his fate. These
scenes of old, hard New England effort, defeated by the soil and
the climate and reclaimed by nature and time — the crumbled,

the lonely chimney-stack, the overgrown threshhold, the dried-up well, the cart-track vague and lost — these seem the only notes to interfere.

The word is "defeated." This country north of Boston ended up more defeated (after Reconstruction) than the defeated South. Southern cotton mills started the decline and fall of the northern mills, and the opened western country took New Hampshire's farms away. Defeat may be melancholy but it creates historians; it provokes connections, while victors (New York, Minneapolis, Los Angeles — and Atlanta) remain trapped in shallow and prosperous modernity.

Neither the New Hampshire dirt nor the dirt of South Carolina extends deep into past time. We dig to find no Roman roads, only artifacts of the nomads who first trudged into this wilderness and hunted bear on these hills or trapped raccoon by these ponds a few thousand years before the Europeans arrived. When we dig in the soil of England, we dig into Stonehenge and Othona, yet England is young compared with the soil of Italy, Greece, Egypt . . . and China! While shaggy Homers improvised hero stories in analphabetic Greece, the Chinese assembled their first dictionary.

How much history does the soul require? Hardy's "indispensable conditions" are "attachment to the soil of our particular spot by generation after generation." How many generations is that? Three is too few; four or five may be sufficient. Let me proclaim Hall's Law: When fifty percent of the local population remain aware of the maiden names of their great-grandmothers, or can visit the graves of ancestors born a century and a half ago, or can tell stories handed down from a hundred years back, the spirit's necessity for connection may be satisfied.

My family's version of Hannah Dustin differs so much from Cotton Mather's that it may derive from another seventeenth- or eighteenth-century ancestor, switched in the telling to the famous name. Of course the truth of it, unascertainable, never matters; the felt connection matters. Another story I remember concerns a male ancestor who fought the French and Indians. Retreating with an outnumbered patrol, my storied forefather volunteered to go back alone through the woods to the abandoned camp in order to retrieve the cooking pot that they had inadvertently left behind. He found it, but on his solitary return he heard the sounds of a war party in the woods. He hid in the hollow trunk of a fallen tree, and moccasined feet pattered over his shelter; he waited, he emerged, he returned safely home. Was the log big enough to hide the pot in? Did he set it upside down on the ground, hoping it might pass for a stump? No one could tell me. When I walk in the woods I look for a rusted pot.

Inhabitants of Danbury, New Hampshire, lack the hunger that citizens of Hamden, Connecticut, feel, and live in an air of connections — with stories of Indian fighters, of famous hermits on Ragged Mountain, of how people built the road through the bog, of how two hundred oxen pulled the mast-tree all the way to Portsmouth, of how the boys marched off to fight Johnny Reb. Connections to the past imply a future. Without past there is no future. If the present's partisan charges that Rusticus "lives in the past" — a sin against America — I claim that only our connection with the past validates the present; the exclusive present is a psychic desert. We Americans pay homage in the church of work to the religion of money and the present, but in our private houses we are despairing atheists. Epidemic despair derives from the violated need for connections. This denial started when we left Devonshire and Calabria, the Norwegian farm and the shtetl in Galicia. We left for good reason. Some connections braid ropes that tie us down; hierarchical structures prevent motion, invention, or discovery, in the name of the fixed relation of part to part, like the planets and the sun that circled the earth. Therefore we sailed two months in an eggshell across the tall Atlantic into a wilderness sparsely populated by a people that, Francis Parkman tells us, regarded us as a source of protein.

But the same forces that shot us loose released the acceleration of energy, which by Henry Adams's law (1904) doubles every ten years. Adams looked back on a life that began with the railroad, doubled into the dynamo's coal energy, and quadrupled toward petroleum with the motorcar and the airplane. Eighty years after the expression of his law, acceleration continues its regular progression. Now the human system — *that lived in one town for five hundred years — generations of stonemasons living on the same cobbled lane to build the cathedral, quiet centuries without technological change — interrupted for slaughter, for Crusade and conquest and Inquisition — has arrived at a panic-present of continual speed, Paris for lunch and New York for dinner, divorce tomorrow in Santo Domingo, and the human system requires pills, dope, alcohol, violence, possibly not greater in quantity, for the quantity has been constant, but violence wonderfully greater in quality; as Henry Adams put it in 1904, "Bombs educate vigorously"* — falters, starves, and dies in the desert of volatility. Against acceleration, Rusticus and its emigrants raise entropy's flag with this strange device, not Excelsior but Lentior: SLOW DOWN.

E. M. Forster's "Only connect" implies a lateral or geographical connection. This good advice works best when the lateral crossing is bisected by a vertical that connects us to the dead, to the old persistent earth of graves and foundations, upward into connection implicit with the divine and the unborn, contracted with the earlier born, earlier flourished, earlier dead. In America outside the historian's library and the antiquarian's museum, the lived past thrives where people live among the dead, separated from the brutality of change, the filmic witness of buildings rising and falling in Hamden, the universe new every thirty seconds.

We are Lentior's vanguard, stewards of human connection. History records no straight lines. As the nuclear plants shut down, let the word go out: *The world of tomorrow is delayed until further notice*. While present-livers expend themselves in acceleration, speed canceling their bodies, let us spend quick lifetimes telling old stories while we stand on dirt thick with the dead.

Rusticus loves deer meat, red flannel hash, the Republican party, the lottery, the Manchester Union, *and his satellite dish. As befits someone of mixed heritage, I cherish half of what Rusticus cherishes and abominate the rest. My love of Lentior has its limits: Who calls me Luddite?*

I ♥ MY DISH

LAST SUMMER we added the latest touch to our old house — to *remain* classic you need to keep up — by installing a twelve-foot satellite dish out back where the saphouse used to be. It's beautiful; we call it our David Smith, although I'm not positive that the sculptor ever worked in black mesh. When I'm eating dinner with my hosts in Idaho, out on a poetry reading, I hand snapshots of my dish around the table; when I come home after my journey I hug it.

Some people think it's strange that I love my dish so much; some people find me inconsistent to love both rural New England and an electronic gadget connected to outer space. Our veterinarian made a rhyme about L. L. Bean flannel watching the Playboy Channel. They ask me how my grandfather would have liked it. Well, I tell them, he would have loved two innings of his Red Sox between supper and shutting up the hens. By 1988, satellite dishes have become the real thing of the country-side — unlike picket fences — as common to backwoods New England as stone walls, yard sales, green shutters, and junkers. If you drive past a handsome clapboard house with a white well-house, a painted barn, and no television aerial, you know that its owners drive up from Boston on weekends in a BMW. On the other hand, over on Route 104 toward Bristol, there's a trailer with *two* dishes in front. After long speculation, I have decided that *she* likes hockey and *he* likes basketball. Ma and pa dishes (double-dip two-scoop) are cheaper than divorces, if *he* goops at a twenty-four-hour Nevada shopping channel and *she* freaks on silent horror movies. In this house I like baseball, I like basketball, I like hockey, and in descending order tennis, soccer, Ping-Pong, volleyball, badminton, lacrosse, boxing, wrestling, arena football, football, roller derby, and golf. The ladder's rungs never give up, and neither does my dish.

At any given moment, this machine can seize something like three hundred alternatives out of thin air: news and news feeds, televangelists, fifty shopping services all flogging the same pink zircon, sitcom reruns, exercise shows, movies — and sports. The movie list in my *Satellite TV Week* runs to five hundred every seven days, but many never get listed. Most interstellar abundance never gets listed, but you develop a feel for what's lurking out there, among spacenuts, spacebolts, and flying saucers — *everything!*

We get French broadcasts from Canada: baseball and hockey, of course, but also European highbrow stuff. We get tons of Spanish. We've discovered a few programs in Italian, one of them various enough to include quiz shows and opera. Once I found a basketball game, small white guys without talent, with announcers speaking an unknown tongue. There's always news in English, not only CNN but the BBC three times a day and network news fed upstairs at three or four different times for the different zones. If you are driven to watch *MacNeil Lehrer* at six, seven, eight, and nine, you can do it.

Mostly I watch live sports. On a Saturday in May I am embarrassed by riches and keep swiveling the dish. There's the NBA on CBS, at one and at three-thirty, on three satellites and four transponders. Because CBS is showing both Denver/Dallas (to most of the country) and Detroit/Chicago (for home folks), I can satellite from one to the other. In the autumn, on a Sunday afternoon, I can find every professional football game as it happens. Summer Saturdays I get NBC's baseball game of the week *and* its backup. Today I pick up the NBA from Telstar 302 because that's near Satcom 4, which is where I catch the Red Sox. I switch around at halftime, between innings, or during time-outs. From one to six I career from Chicago/Detroit to Boston/Seattle to Denver/Dallas. From six to seven-thirty I read a book, because I must conserve sports attention for the Stanley Cup playoffs, Boston Bruins and New Jersey Devils at seven-thirty. Later, if I can stay up so late, the New York Knights take on the Chicago Bruisers at ten-thirty in arena football.

Mind you, this difficult schedule ("When the going gets tough, the tough get going.") occupies me mostly on weekends. Weekdays, unless you care for taped 1978 lacrosse playoffs on ESPN, you often wait until seven-thirty to watch baseball (every night, April to October) or basketball (hundreds of college games, ninety percent of the NBA). But when the Chicago Cubs play at home on weekdays, you can sometimes take in a Cubs game at two-fifteen and a Braves game at five-thirty before the Red Sox at seven-thirty. When my teams play on the West Coast, I can watch an eastern game at seven-thirty or eight before traveling to California for a first pitch or tip-off at ten-thirty. On occasion, I hate to admit, I need to sleep; like everybody else in New Hampshire, I get up at five, and if I've been staring at Anaheim Stadium or the Forum until one in the morning, I feel a little logy by eight A.M. Sometimes during West Coast trips I go to bed at eight o'clock, like everybody else in New Hampshire, and set the alarm for ten-thirty.

If I don't get in these daily hours of sport, my work suffers. When the device was installed old friends worried for me: "They'll say, 'Whatever became of Hall?'" But within a month — about the time of my birthday, when my daughter gave me a T-shirt reading, "I ♥ My Dish" — I had altered my habits. Now I can claim that because of my dish I work twice as much as I did before.

It's a trick, doing a sixteen-hour day, seven days a week, without becoming a workaholic. In order to accomplish this feat, we must placate the It. The It, if you've forgotten, is an internal overseer that the wild psychoanalyst Georg Groddeck described and named, a creature that monitors everything we do. It is powerful, but fortunately It is very, very gullible. To work the hundred-hour week, we must deceive the It, because It needs to think that It's relaxing half the time. When we are young, It thinks that getting drunk is fun, and finds nothing so relaxing as a good vomit; late in life, It may find pleasure in watching *Jeopardy*, or It may read Barbara Cartland or Robert Ludlum. One thing for sure: It demands Its way, and if you don't let It out for a walk, It will burn holes in your stomach. Because I station my It in front of the Boston Celtics (a.k.a. Red Sox, Bruins, Buffalo Chickenwings, Waco Whatevers) eight hours a day, It considers Itself pampered. With Its limited acuity, It does not recognize that between pitches I read magazines, manuscripts by strangers, unsolicited books, today's mail, newspapers, the *Letters of Henry Adams*, my outgoing mail, and page proof; nor does It notice that I floss my teeth, make late revisions in prose, and dictate tomorrow's letters. I used to work from five in the morning until six at night; now I keep going until eleven P.M. Paradise is thinking I'm not working while I work like crazy.

Meantime, I make progress toward the final project, which is to cut out sleep entirely, or at least to restrict it to fifty naps a day, each ninety seconds long and during commercials.

Not that you need to avoid commercials. Often you watch the feed from the arena or stadium to the TV station (known as the backhaul) and catch the game before commercials are added. A year ago I watched no Celtics games, because the away games were on Boston's Channel 56 (which doesn't reach this far) and home games were on cable (which doesn't market itself to a thin population; I get many signals for cable, from all over the country, often by paying a modest annual fee). Now, with my beloved dish, I watch *all* Celtics games; I receive not Channel 56 but the feed to 56 from Phoenix or Cleveland. Among other pleasures, I hear the announcers talk during commercial breaks. Mostly they yell at Louis in the truck or mock a cameraman for attention to cheerleaders, but occasionally I hear athletes described with especial candor.

For backhauls you need to push buttons and feel around in the sky. If you know from the paper that any game is happening anywhere, chances are you can find it, and while you are searching you may find the high school basketball finals from Indiana or spring practice intersquad football from the University of Nebraska. Sometimes it's difficult to know what it is you've found — as the "Bisons," let us say, put it to the "Bulldogs" — but often the ads, if you're getting ads, help you to decipher the signal's provenance. These days, I learn about used car prices in Denver.

With reluctance I will admit that there may be a dark side to dish obsession. It might indicate, for instance, dependence on television, which is of course politically incorrect. It might indicate imbalance, which could lead to immoderate behavior, even to acts of violence. Law-abiding members of the National Dish Owners Association ("Fight Drugs: Buy a Satellite Dish") were shocked last year to read of the fanatic in Connecticut who chopped down his neighbor's oak tree because it blocked his reception. Folks like this ("When Dishes Are Outlawed Only Outlaws Will Have Dishes") make it hard for the rest of us. Newspapers always refer to this fellow as "a self-described television addict," and quote him as saying, "Now I can get the Disney Channel." This vile collapse of morals and judgment ("Satellite Dishes Don't Watch the Disney Channel; People Watch the Disney Channel") may not be blamed on a mere wire-mesh contraption. Now, if that oak tree had been blocking ESPN . . .

The dish sponsors many visionary projects besides the abolition of sleep; I prowl thin air looking for geographical extension. Someday will we stumble on a live hurling match from Ireland, or Moscow Dynamo, or Thai badminton semifinals? I guess not, given the technical differences among video systems; but of course technical problems never tamper with the powers of fantasy. I keep thinking of wandering not only in space but in time.

As it is, we spend the summer in reprises of winter's basketball, and on a cold dark day of December, we find summer's game on half a dozen cable systems. I daydream of going further back, of finding a transponder that carries the young Babe Ruth pitching at Fenway, or maybe John McGraw's Giants wearing black uniforms, or Civil War troops negotiating rules for the developing game. Another possible avenue, open to daydream but cruel to hope, is the channel that gives different results, that shows the game as it ought to have been. On this transponder Calvin Schiraldi strikes out the Mets side in the ninth inning of the sixth game of the 1986 World Series. Or if he doesn't, Bill Buckner fields that grounder neatly and efficiently, the Sox pull it out, and in northern New England we go to sleep happy while New York writhes sleepless in defeat.

But the real question that haunts me: On which satellite, on which transponder, may we discover the future? If only we punch the right combination of numbers and letters, I keep thinking, the dish will grind itself into a new position, blurt some new science-fiction noises, and suddenly we will be watching the seventh game of *next* October's World Series.

The Boston Globe, which I read every morning, excels in columns about the arts. I read essays about singing groups, which I do not listen to, because I like good sentences. The best column is architectural, Robert Campbell's, who will not be persuaded to collect his journalism into a book. (Some writers are more scrupulous than others.) When he asked me to write a column while he was on vacation, I complained of losses.

THE ROOSTER
AND THE SILO

GROWING UP in dense Connecticut suburbs, 1930s and 1940s, I learned to prefer the New Hampshire countryside of my maternal grandparents, sparse and depressed as it was. Coming to Wilmot was time travel, from automobiles back to horses, but I was not a nostalgic ten-year-old. I loved the countryside because it was eccentric, diverse, and various. Neighbors you saw at church or store were old and young, learned and ignorant, fat and thin, shrewd and stupid; they lived in shacks, trailers, and extended farmhouses with or without paint. My suburbs were rows of the same house inhabited by the same family driving the same car.

Diversity persists. On Route 4 near us there's a cluster of old houses where West Andover used to be — five or six, this side of the track — and a great gap where the Viking Inn (Daniel Web-

ster drank there) burned down not long ago. Nearby an abandoned schoolhouse falls in; there's a spruce trailer; there's an
ugly ranch; there's a house that used to be a gas station; there's
a gas station that used to be a house. Uphill off the highway
there's an old Cape in trouble: The roof sags, six junkers sprawl
about it, and a sign says FRESH EGG'S. Here and there a great
old white farmhouse looks south or west, noble and cared-for.
There's a hollow of homemade houses, mostly small and oddly
shaped, different from each other, improvised according to need
and available material. *Architectural Digest* has not run a spread
on them. Each speaks its own accent.

In the hamlet of Potter Place, besides the gingerbread depot
that survives as the Andover Historical Society's museum, there's
an old store that functions as a post office, open four hours a day,
and there's the Potter Place Inn, which a year ago looked teetery.
Because we don't often swoop down the old road, we watched its
revival in quick cuts, like a television ad where they build a house
in thirty seconds. The structure that seemed ready to topple,
shabby on its last legs, squares clean rectangles and returns to
health. Every old building shows diversity over its decades or
centuries, and the direction is not always toward entropy. When
we moved to this house in 1975 we repaired a swaybacked woodshed; we replaced rotten sills and clapboards. Bit by bit we
brought the old place around, and the neighborhood thanked us.
People sent postcards; people came up to us after church.

Not that opinions are uniform in this rural culture, even on
the subject of preservation. There are always some, seeing a
decrepit house, who want to "let the little red rooster run through
it." This rooster burned down "Sabine," granduncle Luther's
cottage. It would have been expensive to fix, but the man who
torched it felt ashamed when he told me. I hold with William
Butler Yeats, who wrote in *Purgatory*, ". . . to kill a house / . . . I
here declare a capital offense." Killing is what we hate, not altering. We added a new room to this house ourselves — and ruined
a roofline. In some protected towns they wouldn't let it happen.
Some of us want zoning, want limits to growth — but we probably don't want the Code Man, villain of Carolyn Chute's *Le-
tourneau's Used Auto Parts*. The Code Man has the social func-

tion of enforcing uniformity. When suburbanites move to the country, they try to outlaw visible poverty. But if all houses in the countryside show green shutters, eighteenth-century lines, and white clapboard, it is no longer the country. It is Woodstock, Vermont.

Mind you, there's worse than Woodstock.

. Twelve miles west of us in New London, diversity drowns under a tide of uniformity as vast homogeneous condos parody the buildings indigenous to the old culture. Residences of a development named Hilltop Place mimic wooden farmhouses with barns attached, painted gray to look paintless but remain tidy. The paintless look refers to poverty, as if poverty were decorative. Many clusters of units include a weird round wooden tower, which, we suddenly realize, makes an allusion to silos. Do Hilltop's inhabitants, retirees from New York and Connecticut, know what silos are for? Marie Antoinette liked to play at milkmaid, but could she muck out a tie-up? Another mass condo, on the New London golf course, called The Seasons, flies uselessness like the flag of its raison d'être. On each side of the entry road, the developers have erected stretches of white wooden fence, curved lateral lines against green grass, as pretty as a picture. But each fence begins and ends unattached, joining nothing, a chalk line without use or function. Even if it were attached, the fence is designed so that it could keep nothing in and nothing out. It is a fenceless fence, a motif, a meandering scalloped icon of decorative vulgar conspicuous waste that mocks the fences and walls men constructed to keep animals out of corn.

Diversity persists, under assault. Bless our trailers, our junkers, and our rotten but redeemable old houses. The real red rooster of this countryside is the designer silo.

CENTURIES OF COUSINS

Last summer I found myself at the historical society of a handsome village in central New Hampshire, near a lake popular with summer people for more than a century. Here were men with white hair and whiter trousers, wearing blue blazers with gold buttons, their faces tanned from tennis, never golf, their grandchildren shiny and polite. Drinking lemonade with an attractive, expensive family, I heard a Boston voice say, "Yes, you see everyone in New Hampshire, but do you notice how you never meet anyone who was born here?"

We have all heard these sentiments spoken of Florida, Arizona, California, Hawaii, and Colorado — islands of drift, holiday, retirement, and suntan; theme parks of the suburban American dream. I was shocked to hear these words spoken about my New Hampshire. But there are many states of New Hampshire, and now I was visiting the resort-state, an important component of New Hampshire's economy (fiscal and cultural) even before the railroads. When America prospered after the War of 1812, the White Mountains became America's Alps, obligatory for the affluent traveler. In the fifteen years before the Civil War, the new railroad invented summer people, vastly increasing the viewers and trippers. The lakes, the favored country towns, and the mountains multiplied their populations tenfold in July and

August. A New Hampshire of dry summer breezes has prospered for a century and a half.

But the state I call my own is a twelve-month place, including mud and mosquitoes. My New Hampshire is the Boston Post cane for each town's oldest inhabitant; it is Old Home Day and the cellarholes that called forth Old Home Day; it is Prize Speaking Day and dressing up as Santa Claus for the elementary school's Christmas program. It is a rural culture derived from postrevolutionary eighteenth-century America.

This society started its decline a hundred and fifty years ago, but in the 1930s its habits still dominated our towns. As it survives now, we still find it in the South Danbury Church Fair. Women work all week cooking casseroles and bread, then toil in the sun on a Saturday afternoon to feed the multitude that line up at four-forty-five. Some who work at the fair grew up in Connecticut or Arkansas, Michigan or New Jersey, but found their way, one by one, to this place that they love. Others — among the men who set up tables and run the auction, among the women who cook — attended Sunday school inside the dark church fifty and seventy years ago.

In the American 1980s, this continuity is almost unthinkable — even if it is a continuity of diminishment. Danbury's population decreased beginning in the 1830s. The hill farms emptied out and citizens struck by poverty moved south to the mills of New Hampshire and Massachusetts, or west to the open spaces of York State, Ohio, Iowa . . . Just now, as our year-round population increases, we begin to equal the numbers of a century and a half ago.

And I fear for the culture's survival. When summer multiplied us by ten for only a two-month season, our society survived and the summer economy helped it; after Labor Day, we went back to being ourselves. Daily life alters when condos crowd with bathers and leafers and skiers and when retirees park Lincolns by the p.o. all year long. Under the assault, the church-supper universe fades. It does not extinguish like a blown candle but diminishes its relative strength, as water soaks salt out of beef. This culture survived the train, the radio, the automobile, and television, but it cannot survive yearlong outnumbering. Our new influx doesn't join the old; its numerousness overwhelms the old and installs in its place the dominant American suburban culture.

For one example only of what passes and what takes its place: Two miles south of us the Potter Place Inn used to be our most popular local restaurant. Everything was family style, too much food well cooked and well served in abundant serving dishes in a barnish room not noted for interior decorating, and the relationship among customers, hosts, and servers was familiar, you might say. The old owners retired and the place has seen its ups and downs. Just recently new people took it over and spruced it up; it looks good now, and the other night we tried it out. The prices have become New Canaan, and so has everything else: The hostess confided that our waitress tonight would be Karen, and Karen asked us if we cared to purchase a beverage.

By definition we Americans are a transient and changeable people; when our company transfers us every four years we cannot grow long roots. Therefore we and our neighbors, looking for something in common, find duplicate bridge instead of harvest festival. Maybe it's trivial to complain when a local institution becomes standard issue. It happens everywhere, even by Eagle Pond, and it's the lack of local variation that we complain of. We settle for Porsches and sailboats because we lack centuries of cousins; improvising a social standard, we make a coast-to-coast etiquette of *Have a nice day*; we purchase beverages instead of buying drinks; because we are changeable, we become interchangeable.

Elderly writers always whine that things have changed. But if losses really happen — and they do — I mean to name the things we lose. Naming is an attempt at preserving.

COUNTRY

MATTERS

Country is the working farm or the farm no longer worked, empty barn presiding over hayfield returning to forest.

country is village or small town set among hills or meadows, on the plain or in the desert.

country is landscape uncluttered with people.

country is an ethic, or an idea, that distinguishes itself from city and suburb.

On the other hand, there is Commercial Country Cute, a parasite that feeds on our genuine collective nostalgia for land, solitude, and rural culture. CCC is a product to be sold and a device for selling other products. To watch television advertising, you would think that America remains a rural nation. Mr. Bartles and Mr. Jaymes (as it were) flog sugarjuice by acting the part of hayseeds. Most egregiously we observe CCC in the marketing of real estate. When the old farmer sells his hayfield under the blue mountain, where he and his forefathers mowed and scythed all summer, the developer bulldozes stone walls and sheds, builds roads, gouges a decorative pond, and erects brown-shingled odd-angled rows of medieval townhouses, called condominiums these days, with access to golf, tennis, and sailboating. Then the developer advertises his units, with layouts in the *Boston Globe* and the *New York Times*, as "Farm Cottage Village Estates" or "Daffodil Meadow Vue Mansions." When the developer names his roads, cut through topsoil constructed out of a century of Holstein manure, the poetics of commerce outdoes itself: "Brown Trout Creek Road," "Blueberry Muffin Lane."

Many consumers who buy these condos, for recreation or retirement, believe or wish to believe that they have entered the world of COUNTRY, when they have purchased only a daydream exploited for greed's sake. Unwittingly they leave Greenwich or Toledo for a place that their own presence, in overwhelming numbers, alters into New Greenwich and New Toledo. For COUNTRY is not merely place or space; it is a culture based on a sparse population and an ethic of liberty. Because our population is small, we can vote to tax ourselves when we attend town meeting. There's no town meeting when your town counts five thousand taxpayers — much less a million. This culture also derives from the natural world, making character subject to the round of seasons and weather. No roof covers the mall of COUNTRY life, making one even climate twelve months a year; we realize human stature under blizzards and beneath mountains.

Condos kill COUNTRY not on purpose but by multiplying citizens past the possibility of intimate citizenship. Where we had villages with outlying farms, we substitute developments with outlying malls — artificial towns with artificial marketplaces. Greed uses nostalgia, fabricating a connection between consumption and COUNTRY. When the new mall rises in Concord, New Hampshire, one motif will be Shaker architecture — ironic homage from the society of commerce to those celibate craftspeople who did not even practice private ownership.

Greed has been with us forever, under the name of avarice, one of the seven deadly sins; it is less often acknowledged that nostalgia has lived with us as long as avarice has. Nostalgia is no sin, but it can be dimwitted, especially when it considers itself a recent phenomenon: *Ah,* moons nostalgia, *back then we were an innocent people, pure, simple, and rural.* Just *when* were we innocent? In 1770 it was 1720; in 1910 it was 1860; in 1990 it will be 1940. For the sixty-year-old of any generation, it was always fifty years ago.

But when it is not dimwitted, nostalgia can be as serious as it is perpetual. City and countryside have been with us always — and city has always regretted loss of C O U N T R Y. Nostalgia appears in the Sumerian epic *Gilgamesh*, a thousand years before Homer. Later, the city-states of Greece depended on outlying farms, and Greek literature regretted separations. Rome at its height squeezed a million and a half people into narrow streets of apartment buildings. The great Latin writers departed Rome for country estates, from which they wrote letters back to the city enumerating country pleasures. Horace's odes celebrated withdrawal to his Sabine farm, by which he separated himself from the bustle and vice of Rome.

The tradition of valuing the rural life over the life of city or court is as ancient as human history. C O U N T R Y is an ethical idea: a place of solitude, meditation, withdrawal, and honest feeling, as opposed to the courtly life of power or the market life of greed. The journey west for Gabriel Conroy in James Joyce's "The Dead," or the journey *North of Boston* for Robert Frost, stands for mental travel to origins and to the genuine — to places of retreat and of vantage from which we make disinterested judgment. In the city — the notion is — under the spur of competition our desires confront crowds of counterdesires, and we do not behave correctly; we lose ourselves to passions of self-aggrandisement: power, wealth, political importance, influence. In the clear C O U N T R Y light, on the other hand, we see without distortion and testify to what we see — unless, I suppose, CCC installs us, in some future generation, on The Farm at Eagle Pond Estates.

When the National Geographic Society planned a book called Discover America, *splendid with color photography and containing the entire United States, they asked me to speak for New England. Editors and author alike understood that the task was impossible; author made sure that editors shared his sense of limitation — and then leapt to accept the task, in the attempt to put together some ideas of history derived from sixty years of looking, listening, and reading.*

MY

NEW ENGLAND

THE COUNTRYSIDE outside my New Hampshire house is the New England we know from postcards and calendars: covered bridges under the blue hills, trees fiery in early October, weathered barns in snow, March's sap buckets hanging from spigots driven into sugar maples, low long farmhouses white with green shutters beside spring's golden daffodils, the green tent of the summer oak. This New England is only a portion of New England, but it is true enough, and so is the poverty that accompanies it, the shacks and the trailers. My New England is the old-fashioned part, north of Boston, and it is this New England that I will mostly write about. Though the suburban culture of General America takes over in the plupart of the six states, New England's past remains frail but alive in the spare countryside.

Summon the mind's map and begin a quick regional survey at the extreme corner of Maine's high Atlantic shores; this land is rough, cold, magnificent, relentless, and underpopulated. The long coast is rocks and lobsters, huge tides, fishing boats, and clapboard houses that age quickly under wind and weather. Inland, the little towns remain crabbed, comfortable without affluence, rough and raw. Enormous forests, crossing westward into New Hampshire and on to Vermont, are the home of loggers and of paper mills that shed their effluents as the wind blows and the waters run. But if we move south in Maine rather than west, driving down the coast following Route 1 and its tributaries to the coastal villages, we come to the summer place, which has occupied coastal and northern New England for a century and a half. The L. L. Bean complex at Freeport, open twenty-four hours a day, is the Vatican City of a mail-order industry that has long since outgrown its homemade signature. The lower coast of Maine is a scar tissue of Holiday Inns, lobster palaces, cottages, and great houses. Only the rich, in protected enclaves, keep the calendar look. When private wealth takes itself to rural New England, to spend itself on summer comforts, it preserves allusions to the past. Our most New England–looking towns survive by infusions of pious wealth from New York and New Jersey, not to mention Iowa and Texas, not to mention Nebraska and Michigan.

Down the coast New Hampshire's brief, dense shore includes Portsmouth, where blocks of old houses, if you shut your eyes to electric wiring, retain vistas of the eighteenth century; it resembles a coastal town in the southwest of England, with clapboard instead of brick or stone. Boston's North Shore encloses the Boston rich. The islands of Martha's Vineyard and Nantucket, like Cape Cod itself, provide daily bulletins from the war between preservation and profit. The coast of Rhode Island, most urban of states, still harbors the cottages and yachts of Newport rich. On Connecticut's shore, Long Island Sound makes the best saltwater swimming of summer, warm and protected, with aeries of wealth and overcrowded public beaches.

Inland in southern New England the factory ruled during the industrial age, spawning great neighborhoods of workers, sponsoring influxes of immigrants to work the machines and eventually to populate the spreading suburbs. Old truck farms five miles outside the cities — New Haven with its guns and Waterbury with its brass; Worcester, Lawrence, Lowell, and Providence with their cotton and woolen mills — turned in the 1950s and 1960s into malls surrounded by ranch houses and, later, by condominiums flattening under the perennial gardens of television antennas. The dominant urban activity altered from manufacturing to shopping.

North of the mall belt, the population has typically varied from season to season. Cape Cod, the islands, southern Maine, and New Hampshire were first to become summer places. Vermont took longer, and as late as the 1950s was less spoiled and ripe for spoiling. Even before the railroad, summer people came to Newport, Martha's Vineyard, and the North Shore, even as far as the White Mountains. Thoreau canoed and hiked; Emerson rode the stagecoach. Romantic sensibilities thrilled to the Byronic swoop of Mount Washington before America's truer alps, westward, opened with the railroad later in the century. In the meantime, trains from Boston took summer people straight to the mountains.

Rural towns engorged for July and August. For a century and a half, the year-round native, farmer or descendant of farmers, has profited from the birds of summer; hill people have mowed grass for flatlanders, cleaned their houses, sold them gas, and cheered when they left. Some native sons and daughters, who gardened and curried and baby-sat and washed Pierce-Arrows, developed a taste for the money they observed; they worked their way through UNH, took a job on Boston's State Street — and turned into summer people themselves.

Survival on north country hill farms was hard work. For one hundred and fifty years, our population steadily dwindled. Exodus began in the early nineteenth century. In 1855 Herman Melville wrote about the "singular abandonment" of the "mountain townships." This diminishment accelerated later, and early in the twentieth century Henry James wrote about farms abandoned in New Hampshire. Even today, as you climb New Hampshire's wooded hills and mountains, you must watch to keep from falling into cellarholes deep in the forest. On the old farm sites, lilacs and roses bloom unseen, once planted and tended by farm wives; everywhere in dense woods you find stone walls that testify to lost pasture, land once cleared by the muscles of farmers. Along disused trails you stumble upon abandoned graveyards.

In 1899 Governor Frank Rollins of New Hampshire decreed Old Home Week, a summer holiday of reunion, when the lost children returned to hills and cousins. Villages put on plays, dances, and church services; they mourned their dead, drank cider, spooned, listened to band concerts, and reminisced. When I first attended these ceremonies in the 1930s, at a Methodist campground in Wilmot — huge pines over tiny cottages and a band shell — nostalgia's energy endured: a longing for home and childhood, a passion of temporary return or reconciliation. The hurricane of 1938 uprooted pines, which crushed cottages. We still celebrate Old Home Day, but no longer do old natives drive here from Ohio or Delaware. The generations that departed died out, and their descendants lack connection. Now the people who return are often summer children who grew up to love the place of rest and exploration. Many new residents of the rural towns are summer people or children of summer people, attracted to northern New England as to another life, an alternative to Brookline or Stamford. They return — at retirement or earlier, by hook or by crook — to field, forest, and stone walls, to ponds and to worn mountains.

They return also to a culture that differs from the society of city and suburb. I emphasize again: Universal to the northern rural parts is the value placed on eccentricity. Every village remembers heroes of strangeness, men and women talked about for decades after their deaths. My cousin Freeman Morrison, dead thirty-five years, is the daily subject of anecdote in my town: how he brought up a heifer virtually to speak; how he moved great rocks with a tripod contraption on the least excuse; how he preferred to work at night and shingled roofs by lantern. This passion for eccentricity provides amusement, which still expresses itself largely in talk, laconic wit ("Have you lived here your whole life?" "Not yet"), and narrative. Most anecdotes are told as true, and New England speech serves purposes of preservation. This cultural convention passes on the tales of the tribe, as our *griots* tell stories and the rest of us listen to remember.

These stories inculcate the culture's ideas of itself — like the story of the ox-cart man, which my cousin Paul Fenton told me. This house could have been the ox-cart man's house, and it has altered with the train and the motorcar. Our rootcellar beams, crudely squared off, still carry bark; when we put in new chimneys in 1976, we piled old bricks, one with the date of 1803. When my great-grandfather expanded the house in 1865, he also built a cowbarn slightly up the hill, away from the house, for safety in case of fire. The house sat on a narrow dirt road. Because the railroad had paralleled the road in 1848, iron power by 1865 had displaced the turnpike's matched teams of horses. Before I was born in 1928, the turnpike (turned into Route 4) had been paved for automobiles. As a boy I watched the last thrust of railroad authority as huge freight trains hauled World War II's steel to Canadian ports. Now, as one hundred and fifty years ago, there is no railroad here — at least there are no trains. The rails that gleamed like sterling in 1943 now rust and flake; bushes and pines push up through dirty crushed stone between pitted ties.

New England, never a single thing, has risen and fallen and changed and remained the same for three hundred and seventy years. No one could have built on the site of our house until after the English, aided by Colonial troops, defeated the French and removed from the Indians their source of muskets and powder. Not far south of us, Salisbury was a prosperous, fortified community by midcentury, but a farmer on its outskirts was liable to be scalped. New England's economy was coastal, as the great sailing ships tracked across the waters to the mother country, to France, to Holland, and to all Europe. There was, of course, the trade in slaves, molasses, and rum. It was not, thank goodness, our only trade. New England's several ports thrived, boiling with the goods of all nations, sailors on leave, and merchants trafficking. Most manufactured goods came from England; we shipped to Europe pig iron, dried fish, tobacco, and white pine, two hundred feet tall, for the masts of the Royal Navy. To the West Indies we carried poultry, beef, and lamb — alive in the absence of refrigeration.

Even today, the culture of the north country derives from people who moved inland from coastal cities to wilderness late in the eighteenth century. The veterans and families who headed for the lonely north selected themselves to work harder than their brothers and sisters, with less comfort, in return for independence. Six Keniston brothers fought in the Revolution, one of them my great-grandfather Ben's grandfather. They grew up outside Boston and after the war scattered north along with thousands of their fellow veterans to the woodlands of New Hampshire and Maine and what would become Vermont.

Paul Fenton's ox-cart man brought the dream of liberty north after the Revolution. This independence was not so much the abstraction of the Declaration — lofty, glorious, and Frenchified — as it was a dream whereby the single unit of a family could exist in benign anarchy without regulation or cooperation. The liberty boys wanted each man his own nation, little city-states in the hills, small valleys dividing narrow units separated from each other by granite.

Separateness from others was not a price to pay but a reward to win. Settlers built rudimentary houses while they cleared ancient trees and moved rocks, making stone walls. Because each family settlement required about forty acres for survival, they could not be crowded. They would never acquire money or save it, but they would contrive their own comfort. The natural world provided wood for warmth and ice for chilling; add a great garden, with a rootcellar for storing apples, potatoes, squash, cabbage, carrots, turnips; add one cow; add deer and turkey shot in the wild, sheep for shearing, maybe flax grown to make linen, bees and sugarbush for sweetness. In this society, men worked in woods and fields while women labored inside at ten thousand tasks. Notions of self-sufficiency became a brief reality — which still creates New England character, in the endurance of its superannuated dream.

The settlers brought values with them north from the coastal cities. They brought the Bible, most of them, and always the *New England Primer*, for education was linked to religion as Protestants required themselves to read scripture. Or, in the absence of religion, education turned almost holy. Out of seventeenth- and eighteenth-century preoccupations came the education industry that remains at New England's center: colleges, not to mention academies. (Rural New England's three major industries are yard sales, skiing, and prep schools.) After the first years of isolation, the settlers cooperated to build schools and churches. Young women, when they stopped studying, taught school until they married; if a New England schoolmarm didn't marry a neighbor, she trekked west. Outside school, education continued in winter parlors as fathers read aloud while mothers sewed in the evening. This society without many books remained ferociously verbal, with recitation its primary form of entertainment. In small New Hampshire towns, children still compete in Prize Speaking Day at elementary schools. In the diffuse centers of rural communities, in villages without even a store, we find a tiny library open six hours a week.

Although government was minimal, it was intense and local. From Massachusetts the settlers brought the town meeting; today we still go over, line by line, all items of the yearly budget. Government by everybody is next best to government by nobody. In sparse areas, everyone takes a turn doing things publicly required. Of course the value placed on local rule produced many Copperheads. If my great-grandfather detested slavery, he claimed that he had no business telling the South how to behave. I have told how this Copperhead fought in the Civil War out of local loyalty, and brought up his children to be Democrats. Thus my cousins are ferocious Democrats swimming against the conservative tide.

The Republican current flows from an eighteenth-century source. Though its headwaters are libertarian — anti-bigness, in government or in commerce — this conservatism votes for big-business Republicans. The individual ethic, in an age of corporations, works toward its own destruction because of its reluctance to restrict the use of land: "If it's your land, you damned well ought to be able to do what you want with it" — even when "you" is a corporation. Increasingly, the brown-shingled, saw-toothed medieval-village-townhouse condos come between the rural New Englander and the mountain he grew up gazing at. The covered bridge is stuffed and mounted; the mountain stream is posted, burdened with ownership; ski slopes sheer where sheep grazed; parking lots blacken the meadow for buses that carry tourists of the red leaf.

·   ·   ·

In the nineteenth century, subsistence farming was already a hard life. On the thin land it was difficult to be provident by saving against the lean years. The Poverty Year of 1816 brought frost twelve months out of twelve and snow even in June, a gift to preachers — though now we know that the agency of God's displeasure was a volcanic eruption in Indonesia one year earlier. Beginning about this time, many children of Yankee farmers left off working the dour land. Mountain villages were abandoned, not for better farmland to the west but for southern mills, a regular wage, and a work week shortened to seventy-two hours. The United States had turned to manufacturing when the politics of war erected embargoes, when privateers and the British Navy shut off international trade. Cities that had been ports now became centers of casting, forging, leather working, weaving, and assembling. New Hampshire and Massachusetts made shoes and cloth — cotton, wool, and linen — while the South supplied raw materials, and New England became the South's England.

Technology also altered the New England farm. Farm machinery beyond the scythe and the pitchfork did not function well on hayfields studded with boulders at a thirty-degree angle. Our ancestors left the hill farms for the valleys, where they could use horse-drawn machinery, and for a while the valley farms prospered. With some flatland for haying, we could milk not one Holstein but six or eight and send our milk by railroad to the city, where mills employed milk drinkers who lacked a mooly cow in the backyard. Many of New England's small, diverse farms survived into the twentieth century, powered by pairs of oxen, by matched teams of workhorses, and by a sprightly mare to pull a buggy. If a farm prospered, the farmer acquired more land.

Along with land, education remained a value. Ben Keneston's daughter, my grandmother Kate, took the train five days a week to Franklin High School — six years of Latin and four of Greek. When Kate married Wesley Wells, he moved in and farmed with his father-in-law. Their three daughters — my mother Lucy the eldest — also took the train to Franklin High, and then the train to faraway Bates College in Lewiston, Maine, where the girls met the rest of New England. My father, who went to Bates from a suburb of New Haven, took Lucy to Connecticut, and thus I grew up in another New England, four miles from Yale University. New Haven, over two centuries, had translated itself from a port to a manufacturing town. By the late 1920s, when I was born, Hamden resembled the suburbs of Providence, Boston, and Portland. The house I grew up in was solidly made in a neighborhood of similar houses with six rooms, a small yard, and a garage. If the houses were alike, so were the children, the fathers and mothers, the dogs and cats. But in 1936, when we moved in, Spring Glen in Hamden still felt raw; farms remained visible underneath the tidy city blocks.

Or underneath my Connecticut grandfather, who appeared to be a businessman. My father's father, Henry Hall, was born and grew up only blocks away from our house, born in a time when there were no blocks but only the acres of Farmer Webb. Henry's father, Charlie, another Civil War veteran, worked as Webb's farmhand, among other tasks delivering milk to Webb's neighbors. Late in his life Charlie quarreled with the boss, quit the job, bought milk from another farmer, and continued delivery, his son Henry working with him, adding customers. When Charlie died, Henry expanded the dairy and joined up with the Brock family; together they built the great brick factory of the Brock-Hall Dairy in 1935. The business grossed millions of dollars in the early 1950s, but a decade later it had wasted away to nothing — its bigness the usual victim of a greater bigness, not to mention the automobile and the use of milk as a supermarket loss leader. My grandfather died at ninety-one, a widower supported by the utilities he had bought when the going was good, living bewildered in a suburban house on land where, as a boy, he had picked strawberries, ten cents an hour, for Farmer Webb.

When in the 1930s and 1940s I traveled from Hamden to New Hampshire, I moved not only from one New England to another but from one century to another; New Hampshire's farms were not agribusiness. When we went north in the Studebaker, we passed industrial poverty on the journey to rural poverty. In Massachusetts and Rhode Island, as in Connecticut, hard times were closed mills with men idle on street corners. In New Hampshire the farming depression had preceded the general debacle by a decade, starting just after the Great War. For a century the valley farmer had pursued his chores with the aid of hired hands; now he struggled alone. He could work on the road to pay his taxes, and because he had not borrowed money, he avoided foreclosure. But he was poor, and the valley farms came to resemble the subsistence hill farms of the century before: They produced food and warmth but no cash.

A few farms specialized in one crop — apples, strawberries — and thrived or at least survived. Mostly the aging farmers let their places go, and the white houses turned gray. Where matched teams and oxen thrived three decades earlier, one bony old horse pulled buggy, mowing machine, rake, and hayrack. Lacking help from men or oxen, the farmer gave up his poorer fields to bush and pine. More cleared land returned to forest every year, and the landscape moved backward from the nineteenth century to the eighteenth. Population continued to drain away, only reversing itself in recent decades. In the land boom of the seventies and eighties, even Melville's "mountain townships," emptied in the 1850s, started to fill up again. Some towns have regained their peak population of the 1830s but with a difference: Then, isolated families farmed subsistence acreage; now, retirement condos and vacation lodges crowd the lake.

I remember the field I first hayed, the summer of 1939. My grandfather was cutting a patch of stout hay a mile north of us on Route 4, widow hay from a field with no man left to farm it, and he had cut it and let it dry for two rainless days. Because this was the big day, we made it a ceremony. My grandmother packed a picnic lunch. My aunt Caroline was visiting with her car, and at noontime we joined my grandfather in the fields, spreading a cloth over the grass under an apple tree at the edge of the hayfield, eating sandwiches and hard-boiled eggs and custard pie washed down with milk and coffee.

When we had eaten and tidied up, the two women drove home with the debris. My grandfather lay on the grass under the apple tree and closed his eyes for a minute. Then he commenced raking with the horse-drawn rake, and when the piles were completed, he pitched hay onto the rack and I cleaned up the site, using the bullrake. This instrument was four feet across with

tines ten inches deep and a long, bent handle; you walked pulling the bullrake behind you. Later I would take instruction in
pitching-on and in loading the hay on the rack and treading it
down, but now he did the heavy work while I learned not to
catch the bullrake in a woodchuck hole and break a tine. We
made hay as farmers had done for a hundred years. On the slow
ride home he told stories. At the house my grandmother pumped
fresh well water, frosting the sides of a pitcher. The cloth of this
anecdote unravels swiftly: When I drive past the hayfield now,
it has grown up to stout trees, not only fir and birch but hard-
wood.

The countryside outside my New Hampshire house remains
beautiful: Mount Kearsarge in its glory changing with the seasons, pasture with intact stone walls growing magnificently into
forest, and population still sparse, independent, and eccentric.
But if we imagine the future of my old hayfield-turned-wood-
lot — and if population continues to increase, if we avoid plague
and war — maybe we see neither woods nor fields but blocks of
houses crowded together, like my Connecticut grandfather's suburbs risen over the strawberry fields — and the countryside of
New England gone, gone, gone, preserved only in paintings or
photographs and in old books.

Our passion for eccentricity, as I take it, expresses itself largely in talk. Not only eccentricity: also the melancholy of aging, the passion of interest, the losses of change — and the banality of the ordinary. Doubtless listening is the largest source for my writing. To end these notes from Eagle Pond, I gather fifty voices together. This prose, discriminated into a genre, would call itself fiction. When we rely on a tape recorder, we write fact; when we rely on memory exaggerated by imagination, we write fiction. I made up all the names.

FIFTY PEOPLE
TALKING

Rena Guptil: "Didn't use to be many come by that road. Drummers, sometimes, and Mrs. B. she kept two rooms over the front where they could sleep if they'd a mind to. Long about after the war, times nobody moved in and just about everybody moved out, 's when she closed up. That and the rheumatism. Now I don't know where they come from, cars all over the road day and night, seems."

Samuel Weare: "Oh, when he was a boy he was different all right, but not so much different as he turned out later. His grandfather let him raise that ox and he named him Perfect. He wanted to take Perfect to school with him, they was that close."

Morris Giannelli: "I felt bad about it ever since. Now Eben he was some uncle to you? I felt bad about it ever since. He was dead before we got here, we never knew him, we never had no use for the house, just the land come with it that we used for the campgrounds, so we rented Eben's place out. Always troubles with the tenants. Finally these Campeaus, no-goods, they took off middle of January owing rent for two months, not telling nobody. It was cold, thirty, thirty-five below, and by the time I knew they was gone pipes was busted and then it thawed and then everything got soaked. Oh, it was a mess, you never saw . . . I got disgusted I guess, and I felt bad about it ever since, but I did it, then. We didn't have no insurance on it. I let the little red rooster run through it."

Betsy LaFlamme: "May took to herself after Roy died. They was mostly to themselves *before* he died, I suppose, but after the funeral — she went to the funeral, they wasn't many that did — she stopped coming to town for groceries. We figured Carl brought her a bunch when he stopped by. The last five years she never picked up her mail. Of course she never paid the town no matter how they dunned her. When Sherman was selectman he tried . . . but she wouldn't come to the door. At town meeting they wouldn't let Sherman put her house up."

Marcus Major: "When I saw Wes down to the store I probably grinned. I used to jaw with him when I sold him cordwood. 'Hell,' said Wes, 'I saw something about you in the paper.' I said, 'Well, you're likely to run into me any old place. I'm all over the place.' 'Yep,' said Wes, 'just like horseshit.' "

Jimmy Bucyk: "Did I tell you about when Wash had his teeth out? They was bothering him some, mostly in the spring, and one day he says, 'Jimmy, can you drive me to Doc Smith's?' When we got there I parked right in front, not like today, across from Holmes and Nelson's, Western Auto's there now, and he told me wait. Wasn't gone more than fifteen minutes. Doc Smith proposed to give him the needle but Wash said don't take the time. He came out of there with some cotton wadded up to his mouth but by the time we was home there wasn't no more bleeding and Wash was gabbing away like always."

Sharon Sherman: "We never had anybody murdered before. I know Billy Chasen blames himself, letting old Pod keep the station open late. Pod liked it late at night, you know, nobody ever bothered him and he kept the radio going. Radio was still going when Chasen found him at five the next morning, lights on, cash box open. They took the pennies, Chasen said, they took the pennies even . . . Chasen says he knows who done it but they can't do nothing."

Bruce Humble: "When they opened him up they was cancer all through him. Of course they let the air in, so it grew real fast. That cancer took him real quick."

Anson Stewart: "Lincoln Bascomb wasn't much for doing chores. When his stove went cold he chopped more birch - birch burns green, you know that? — and took off just enough logs to fill the firebox. He'd be out there with his saw before it was light on a cold morning. Sometimes he brought his hay in with snow on it. He planted corn in July so he never did take it in. Every few years, to pay his taxes, he'd sell off some more of his daddy's land."

Lester Ford: "Tuesdays when I made the run from Berlin I stopped to see old Chester. He smoked a pipe then and didn't that trailer fill up with blue smoke! Every week he remembered a new story. My, he could tell stories, even when he couldn't hardly move, his leg was so bad. When I got up to leave, he always said the same thing: 'Told you a lot of lies.' "

Martha Bliss: "It was hard to keep track but it was something like this: Old Herbert was married to Lois, I suppose twenty years ago, but she already had Yvonne, brought her with her, I suppose, and sometimes her boyfriend Hector stayed with them, at least folks said so, I suppose, and when Yvonne started to swell up, I suppose Lois said it was Herbert but Yvonne said it wasn't and that's when she married Lonnie but he hadn't been around town long enough."

Mark Brown: "I heard Lila telephone Bertha even though their houses wasn't fifty feet apart. 'Bertha,' she said, 'go look at the sunset,' she said. 'It's pretty as a picture postcard!' Lila saw beautiful things every place she looked. I told her she rose her eyes up so high she couldn't tell she was stepping in shit. Hah-hah."

Johnny Buso: "At Blackwater Bill's, late August, after the first hard frost, old Lebow limped in to set at the counter two stools down from old Peter, took the coffee mug that Stacey handed him, and turned to Peter and asked him, 'How did your garden fare?' "

Polly Shepherd: "One thing about Lulu you could be sure of, she'd never tell you a thing straight out. If she was down to church playing the organ and you asked her wasn't it Sunday, she couldn't tell you just so. Why, I remember one day we was standing under the awning down to Henry's store, and the rain it was pouring down, and I asked her, 'Lulu, do you think it looks like rain?' 'Well,' she said, 'I guess maybe, might could be, maybe perhaps.' "

Chester Ludlow: "They was always rowdies here. If they didn't live in town they came to town to do their mischief. Halloween they piled gates and washing machines and motorcycles, even a snowmachine, right up in the square where their granddaddies used to stack outhouses."

Lucy Banks: "Papa died thirty years ago but I still say that's where I live, Papa's house. People don't stop by the dooryard the way they used to. Used to, it was the horse and buggy for some of them, Model T or Model A for most. Some are dead now I suppose. Most."

Edna Best: "Everybody worried what Thelma'd do when Edward died. She couldn't drive and her daughter'd gone down to

Rhode Island someplace, but then Thelma died first — we never could of believed it if we hadn't seen her there up to Melton's at the viewing, she just didn't seem like the kind to die — and Edward cooked for the fair, rolls and two casseroles and pineapple upside-down cake, the way Thelma'd done it."

LeRoy Wallace: "He came from the city, I know that much, down Massachusetts way, a flatlander but not like the most of them I guess. Didn't want to have much to do with anybody, never went to town meeting much less church or the Grange. We obliged him."

J. G. McNair: "I knew both your great grandfathers. How do you like that? John Wells he was the blacksmith talked funny, what do they call it, cleft palate. Other was old Ben Keneston used to drive his sheep twice a year, fall and spring, down the Bog Road. Something to see, those four hundred sheep."

Hunnah Robey "I used to sit on that porch with a man born 1850 and he told me about how the children, him and his sisters, told their father go hide because the drafting man was coming. Don't seem like I'm old enough to remember somebody remembering the Civil War. I guess I am. Old enough."

Lucille Huntoon: "That was when they still kept the pool hall, right down the street from the state liquor. Academy boys, they used to sneak into the pool hall, they wasn't supposed to, and pay somebody fifty cents go buy them a pint of William Penn. Lots got sent home. State of Maine Express came through here every night. Some teacher would put the boy on the train, telegraph his daddy he was coming home, want him or not."

Bertha Butts: "Hamilton was the market town back then. Friday nights they stayed open and Loren would drive us there, fifty cents both ways. Oh, it seemed like a big place then with the Newberry's and the Woolworth's both and the old A & P. You should have known it then."

Ralph Gallo: "At town meeting our road agent talked about needing new equipment, talked for much as half an hour. He keeps the roads good. Bob our moderator, he called for a vote. 'Everybody wanting to buy William his new front loader?' "

George Paradise: "The Greek made that diner with blue-plate specials forty-five cents for meat loaf or chicken croquettes and mashed and two vegetables, bread and butter too. Never knew what happened to him. One day and he's gone, no more Greek."

Eddie McCarthy: "Met this fellow from York, Maine, and he says, 'I seen you somewheres before,' and I says, 'I never seen you before in my whole life,' and he says, 'Did you ever catch a fish? A big haddock? Up in York, Maine?' And I swear, I couldn't believe it. I'd forgot, it's true, first time ever I went deep-sea fishing I caught that fifteen-pound haddock, they took my picture and he seen it. Way up in York, Maine."

Forrest Mack: "When they started digging for the landfill I said to Sherm, 'Ain't that where we used to went skating?' 'Still do,' said Sherm. 'You ever seen them dig a landfill except where there's groundwater?' Sure enough by July the Jack Wells Brook looked like swill. Sure enough by August there wasn't a minnow left in Eagle Pond. Where was the state water folks when the brains was handed out? Sherm says they was out behind the Grange getting paid off."

Lucy Bates: "We moseyed over to her house about four o'clock, she's got that new trailer over on Treatment Plant Road, so's we'd be there time for kickoff. Turned out, nobody watched the game anyway. Super Bowl or not. Turned out, nobody there'd seen a game all fall. She had a dish, the picture was real good, but we just talked. John Johnson he stood right in front of the set, couldn't see anything if you'd of wanted to."

Rex Mumford: "There was two places in Hamilton you could get a drink, right next door to each other. When my Aunt Maybelle — she's the one had a car, schoolteacher, only car in the family — took me downtown with her, she lifted her nose when we drove past either one. They was called Eagle Tavern and Freddie's Bar and Grill, both gone now, but Maybelle was afraid, you see, she'd see her own brother come falling out."

Margery Tibbets: "On the common, there in the village — that stone, that's the soldier boys went off to all the wars. Some names you wouldn't believe, yard-sale names, was up to Canada back before we was a country, up fighting the Frenchmen. Lots in the Civil War, your great-grandfather too. Not so many in 1917. There wasn't so many around by 1917."

Jeff Getz: "Forty years that old place stood there with nobody in it. They kept shingles on it but they wouldn't sell it because they fought over who got the property after old Prescott died. It's on a back road, gravel, so I didn't go there in the winter but I liked driving past it when the weather was dry. Good old stone walls over that way, never tumble, and Gambier's place is real pretty, and there's a pretty field. Well, every spring I was half scared to go there, for fear the roof'd fallen in after a snowstorm. Then Miss Borders she bought it, my goodness, and bit by bit she brought the old place back. I bet it didn't look any better a hundred years ago."

Audrey Hoop: "Johnny was always a good boy but not too smart I suppose. When he got himself married it seemed like something just switched on: 'Time to get married!' He married Hildy because she's the first girl he saw after the notion switched on. Lots of us knew what she'd been up to but Johnny didn't. Then he got drafted and went to Vietnam and when he got home he found out what Hildy'd been up to — he couldn't miss it, no matter what; what she'd been up to was one month old — so he signed up for another tour and that's when it happened."

Hamp Lebow: "You knows that house down by Buffalo's old camp? Where they used to be the pink mailbox? Don't go near there if you can help it. When I sell light bulbs for the Lions, I knock at every place but I don't knock there. Fellow there's so mean he shoots cats.' "

Stella Budge: "I taught forty years in that school, one room, anywheres from eleven to twenty-seven scholars at a time, and Percy was the smartest I taught in all those years. When he was six years old I said to Mr. Hubbard, 'You see that little blond one? You remember: He'll be selectman!' "

Martha Musgrove: "When Emily died it was as if the blood dried up in everything — in school where she worked with the kids that had troubles, in church where she went every Sunday for sixty years, even in her family, that began to pull apart then. Everybody wondered for years what flowed them together because they was Republicans and Democrats, cops and crooks together."

Martha Bates: "He was always filling in those ads they print inside paper matches: *Complete High School. Earn $20,000 in Spare Time. Get Big Money Working for Airlines. Drive a Tractor Trailer. Read Palms.* I brought him the mail when they was too much snow and he couldn't cross the meadow to the p.o. I bet I brought him one thousand Informative Treatises."

Lucy Popovich: "Mrs. Roberts, she knows where the wild strawberries are. Before that, she's picked asparagus from the side of the road. Later the blackberries and blueberries. She knows a mushroom from a toadstool. You see her, May to September, walking beside the road with her neck crooked over from the rheumatism and a basket over her arm. She knows where everything grows. Where everything *is*, that grows."

Danny Dumaine: "Lloyd and Andrew been running their gas station fifty years. Andrew can't promise anything. 'Going to do that oil change this morning, Andrew?' 'I suppose, might do, if we get lucky, if nothing happens.' But Lloyd now, he's different. He has his sayings. When you're about to drive off, Lloyd'll say, 'Drive like hell, you'll get there.' "

Billy Little: "Nothing went right for Belle. She stayed with her old father because nobody else would and all he done was crab at her all day and all night for twelve years until he died. Then she took up with that fellow from Manchester — *said* he was from Manchester — but then one day he was *gone.* They said he had a wife come and get him."

Betsy Wells: "When I was a little girl I sat on the porch with Elzira my grandmother's sister. She taught a one-room school down by the old Campgrounds for forty years. Elzira, she never got married. They said she was too particular. Mostly she stayed down to her cottage, but she liked to walk up to my grandmother's house for gossip. She knew everything and she never missed church. 'Why did God make hornets?' I asked her. She said in the olden days people used hornets for rheumatism. She said I should be a lawyer when I grew up."

John Johnson: "He never had any money. If he had any money he bought land with it. Land-poor, he was. In 1916 he put up five hundred gallons of syrup. You know how much sap that takes? Forty to one, most years. Sold them for a dollar a gallon and bought two hundred and twenty acres. Huldah still sewed underwear out of flour sacks. Mind you, if they'd *had* some money, Huldah would've thought it was a shame to waste good flour sacks."

Betty Gould: "Parker grew up here, sure, right where he lives now on Parker Mountain Road, where they don't have a mountain, but he never was one to mix much, back then, when he was a boy. So he went to college someplace and then I guess down to New York City and thirty years later he comes back to stay, right back to the old place stayed closed up after his daddy died. Of course when he comes back he's got this fellow George with him. People say things but I don't see as they make any bother."

Lucy Little: "Bob Smith kept that store for twenty years. Go there at six in the morning or six at night, Bob stood there smiling at you in his short sleeves. He was like the mayor, if we had a mayor, and a good sight more agreeable than any selectman we ever had, I'll tell you. He liked it, running the store."

Annie Parsons Whitfield: "We met Tuesday afternoons, first and third Tuesdays, and we *did* sit in a circle and we *did* do quilting. Must have gone on sixty years or more, my grandmother went with her grandmother. When Martha Bliss moved in down to the old store, that was the end of it. She talked so mean. Nobody wanted to come anymore. What a shame."

Herbert McNeilly: "I worked on the roads five years when old Mansfield was road agent. Oh, my. Old Mansfield he took the town for plenty, I'll tell you, and the town voted him back in every March just the same. Old Mansfield drove the dump truck and *always* had a six-pack riding shotgun I don't know. When he quit — yep, he *quit* — the town found they was something like ten thousand gallons of gas not accounted for. They was nothing to do about it."

Sherman Buzzle: "You want *zoning* you go to Russia, back to Russia."

Loren White: "The old Rialto down to Hamilton, I remember when they built it, bad times and nothing much else got built then. That was when them CCCs camped up on the hill and built the park they call, what?, Whitmore State Park. It holds up. We used to get free dishes Monday nights and a double feature too. Seems like it cost fifty cents. Course that was ten gallons a dollar times."

Bunch Havelock: "Look at old man Gossage, you'd never think he'd been anywhere but that trailer out by Wells Creek. The age he was, though, they'd all been somewhere. I guess! He don't talk much but once down to the firehouse, they had some beer, and he told how they flew sixteen, eighteen hours in those little old airplanes — B-24s? 25s? They wasn't 747s, I'll tell you. Well they took off from some little island or other, nothing but an airstrip and a beer hall, where the Marines got killed on those invasions, Tarawa and Iwo Jima, burning Japs out of their caves. Well, they flew eight, ten hours all across the Pacific and dropped bombs on them paper houses, Japan. Tokyo I guess. They could see the fires a hundred miles off, when they flew back, eight, ten hours back. Can you imagine that? Old Gossage the gunner."

Jane Johnson: "Town meeting got a little rough that year. Andy Bascomb got into a fistfight with Sherman Buzzle and of course the moderator would of usually got the constable to throw them out but Andy was moderator and Sherm was constable."

Bob Smith: "People'd come in here, or I'd go pump gas, they wouldn't — they *couldn't* — take off without they told me some story. Didn't matter what, just so it was some story. Some, they'd tell half a dozen. I didn't mind. I told them right back, to somebody else, keep them circulating like a dollar bill. Come bedtime was the only time the stories stopped. Good night."

Martha Ludlow: "I get so tired of politics! Chester don't talk about nothing else unless it's taxes, and what's the difference? I wish he'd got elected selectman that time, get it out of his system. Sherman Buzzle beat him. Seven votes. That was just before I had the appendix."

HERE AT EAGLE POND

*was typeset by Heritage Printers in Linotype Waverley,
a face based on the designs of Justus Erich Walbaum, a
nineteenth-century German typefounder. The woodcut
illustrations by Thomas W. Nason were reproduced from
prints in the collection of the Boston Public Library. The
book was designed by Anne Chalmers and was printed
and bound by The Book Press, Brattleboro, Vermont.*